MW01047252

To Gay,

So great to meet
you — looking
forward

GREEN FLASHES AND to
next Time!
GOOMBAY SMASHES

Cindy
Shearer
Water Island
Feb 2017

Green Flashes and Goombay Smashes

Life, Death and Sunsets

Cindy Shearer

Print information available on the last page.

Rev. date: 10/19/2015

To order additional copies of this book, contact:
Xlibris
1-888-795-4274
www.Xlibris.com
Orders@Xlibris.com
709622

DEDICATION

For Mom:

With love and gratitude for encouraging me to follow my dreams

and

With hope that in some small way, I have honored your last wish, by keeping alive the important dialog surrounding end of life issues.

CONTENTS

INTRODUCTION

Around her 90th birthday, Mom started talking matter-of-factly about her death. Until then, she spoke of it occasionally, mostly worrying aloud how she would juggle her two deceased husbands in the next life.

"It's heaven, Mom," I told her. "They have it all figured out."

She'd give me a skeptical look, and continue to fret.

Otherwise, thankfully, Mom said little on the subject.

In April 2014, the whole family gathered for Mom's week-long 90th birthday celebration. In contemplating how three generations had traveled from near and far for her big event, Mom casually remarked that it was too bad she hadn't died. Her reasoning was that since we were all together anyway, it would be a convenient time for her memorial service. Ever practical, the concept of killing two birds with one stone was right up Mom's alley (to borrow two of her many clichés). Fortunately, I don't think Mom phrased it quite that graphically. Still, the topic was never far from her mind, which was a bit unsettling.

The family assured Mom that we were happy to be together to celebrate her 90th birthday, and not for a more somber occasion. Little did we know that before the year was out, we would indeed gather again to celebrate Mom's life, this time without her. Come to think of it, we did kill two birds with one stone—Mom died on December 1st, and we waited until we gathered at Christmastime to hold her memorial service. Mom would no doubt approve; perhaps some of that practicality wore off on her children.

Speaking of her children... since this is the Introduction, I guess I should introduce us:

Here we are with Mom on her 90th birthday on Captiva Island, one of her favorite spots. As you can see, there are four of us: three boys and me. Scott, Lance, Cindy and Kirk, in that birth order. (We are pictured from right to left.) The Fearsome Foursome, Mom sometimes called us, or The Fabulous Four. Scott and Kirk live in Sparta, New Jersey, Lance lives in Naples, Florida and I live in the Virgin Islands.

Mom was born (Dora) Adele Kuntz in 1924, became Adele K. Shearer in 1946 when she married Donald Shearer, our Dad, and became Adele K. Scully in 1974 when she married our Step Dad, Jack Scully, after Dad's death. Mom lived in Naples, Florida.

Here's another shot from that 90th birthday week. As you can see, the Fearsome Foursome has grown. The boys have wives (Alicia, Lynn and Sharon, respectively). Scott and Alicia have three daughters (Jessica, Jaclynn and Rebecca); Lance and Lynn have two daughters (Dana and Carly); and Kirk has two step-children (Michael and Kimy). We've also added some more males: Jaclynn's husband Matt, Dana's husband Ryan and Becca's husband Jason. (In case you are counting, not everyone appears in the photo). This occasion also marked Mom's introduction to her first—and only—great grandchild, Belle (Matt and Jaclynn's daughter). That's Belle on Mom's lap. They were a sight to behold.

Mom's 90ᵗʰ birthday week was a whirlwind of varied and wonderful activities: meals out, sunsets, boating, picnicking, beaching, touring; never a dull moment, as Mom might say. Mom loved being on the go and, despite the fact that by then she was virtually deaf (we communicated mostly on a white board), blind in one eye, and pretty much confined to a wheelchair, she rallied for the festivities.

Here's the note she wrote to us on her white board at the end of that week:

> Thanks to every one of you for coming so far and going to so *very* much trouble to bring this all together. It's been a great life and produced a fabulous family. Look around you. Spouses, too. Sorry that I am not in top shape to contribute to all the celebrations. But wasn't it all worth it just to behold Belle (the Clapper), my very first and fantastic great granddaughter. Love you all more than I can say–Mom

At the time, Mom was living by herself in an "independent" apartment in a senior living community that she and Jack moved to in 2006, after living on their own had become a little "wild and woolly," as Mom described it in her Christmas card that year. TCG is an upscale facility whose common areas look more like a hotel than an old folk's home. Mom and Jack's unit was a small one bedroom, which Mom dubbed "The Mouse House." In addition to the bedroom, it had a living room/kitchen area, and a small balcony. The balcony is what sold them on the place. "Look!" Mom would announce, swinging open the balcony door. "The whole world's out there!"

That was incredibly important to Mom; forgive the cliché, but the world was her oyster. Always aching to know what lay around the next bend, Mom spent her first eighty-plus years exploring as much of the globe as possible. Here's an overview of her life, taken from Mom's obituary:

Born Dora Adele Kuntz in 1924 in Hunters Run, Pennsylvania, Adele was one of the original snowbirds. Beginning when she was three, Adele's family made the long journey from Pennsylvania to Clearwater, Florida every winter because of her grandfather's delicate health.... Adele married Don Shearer in 1947 and they headed for Cambridge, Massachusetts, where Don was a student at Harvard Business School. Over the next several years, she juggled her husband's blossoming business career with the raising of their four children. In 1963, Don landed a job with Colgate-Palmolive International, and off the young family went on an around-the-world adventure, making their home in Australia, Hong Kong, and the Philippines. While living overseas, Adele continued to nurture not only her children but those less fortunate. In Hong Kong, she taught English to the children of Chinese fisherman—on the rooftop of an eighth-floor walkup building.

Adele's globetrotting led her to Naples in the early 1970s...After Don died, she married Jack Scully, who worked for Pan American World Airways, and the globetrotting continued.

Adele literally traveled around the world, and visited every continent except Antarctica. After retiring, her adventures continued aboard *Moonglow*, the boat that Adele and Jack called home for a few years as they cruised the waters of the Pacific Northwest, the Gulf of Mexico, the Bahamas and the Caribbean. Adele and

> Jack eventually found their way back to
> Naples, where Adele continued to enjoy
> traveling, boating, and her kitty, Tiva.

Small wonder, then, that it meant so much to Mom be connected to the world via that balcony. She and Jack decorated the Mouse House with treasures gathered from around the globe, and settled into their new home, along with Tiva, their cat. With the exception of some "blips" here and there, Mom and Jack had several good years in the Mouse House. They enjoyed dressing for dinner in the TCG dining room and participating in activities—from exercise class to ice cream socials. They especially liked the guest lecturers who spoke about world affairs.

Mom and Jack outside TCG Christmas 2008

Mom's curiosity about the world and desire to broaden her horizons never wavered; long after her traveling days were over, Mom would scour the atlas to find a place she'd read about in her newspaper, which she read religiously. Scattered throughout the Mouse House were notes she'd written to teach herself world capitals, leaders and other names that would pop up in the news.

"Ulaanbaatar," Mom would repeat, over and over. "Why can't I remember that?"

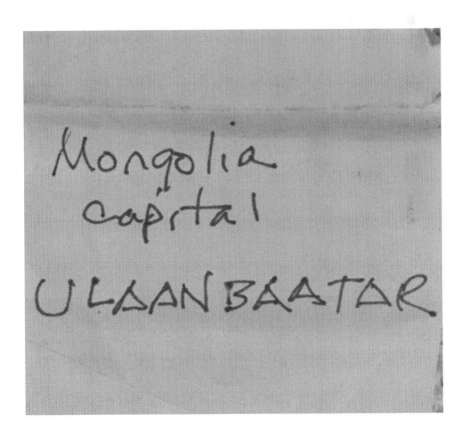

Mom also puzzled through an increasing number of topics in the newspaper that were foreign to her in another sense.

"Cindy," she asked, "What is blog, what is bling, and who is Sponge Bob Square Pants?"

It was harder and harder for Mom to keep up but, characteristically, she did her best.

Always one to "roll with the punches," as she would put it, Mom took her aging in stride. When adult onset hydrocephalus robbed Mom of her balance, she chose the sportiest three-wheeled walker she could find, dubbing it her Harley. Lance added the appropriate decals, and she kept on rolling. Mom tackled arthritis, urinary tract issues and many other maladies with equal aplomb. Hearing aids initially helped Mom's hearing loss, although eventually, she would lose all hearing in her right ear, and 90 percent of that in her left. This was tough, because Mom never lost even one percent of her inquisitiveness.

As her own heath declined, it was increasingly difficult for Mom to care for Jack, who was also failing. Eventually, Jack was transferred to a nearby skilled nursing facility, where he died in August 2012, at age 92. By the end of his life, Jack was bed ridden and loopy, in part because of pain medicine. Stenosis caused his feet and legs to turn black from lack of circulation. It was hard to watch this hands-on, "no problem," easy-going man become so feeble. ("The guy I'd most want to have on a desert island," Mom gushed in their courting days about her "Mr. Wonderful"). There was no doubt in our minds that the Jack we knew would be appalled at his end-of-life circumstances. He had signed the "Do Not Resuscitate" orders and similar advance directives, yet these could not prevent a slow, painful death that was hard on everyone.

By the end, all of us, including Mom, were hoping and/or praying for Jack's life to be over; yet, mentally changing gears to embrace death rather than life can be difficult. Mom visited Jack often, making the long walk with her Harley down the corridor to his room.

"I wonder if they are weighing him?" she'd ask, after a visit. "It looks like he's losing weight. Do you think he's getting enough to eat?"

Yet later, she'd say, "There are only so many beds, so many nurses," explaining that she worried that someone who could be getting better was not because finite resources were going to Jack instead, to sustain a life that was not worth living.

Mom and Jack on their 25ᵗʰ wedding anniversary trip to Napa Valley 1999

Mom rallied for a time after Jack's death. Although her hearing was worsening and her declining balance caused her to give up the three-wheeled Harley for a more stable, four-wheeled model, Mom characteristically put her best foot forward and kept chugging along. She always dressed impeccably, even if she wasn't leaving the Mouse House. Mom loved shoes and, although she'd had to forgo some of her favorites because of her "wobbliness," Mom still managed to sport snazzy footwear while most of her compatriots made do with sneakers or slippers. Till the end, Mom polished her own nails and they, too, were impeccable.

"Do all the women at TCG hate her?" joked a friend.

After her death, Mom was universally remembered as "sparkling"— being "classy and snazzy" as one of my closest friends from junior high school days put it. Perhaps that friend's mother summed it up best: "Adele was always so full of life. I remember the day we took Adele and Don to the airport, hoping he would be able to get on the plane to Florida. He was very sick. Adele was painting her nails. I was biting mine."

Here's Dad, in healthier times, as Skipper of our first boat, The Booty, in the early 1960's

Eventually, Mom became almost completely deaf. I recall sitting with her at Unity Church one Sunday. For awhile, the headsets the church provided helped but, as her hearing worsened, it was tougher and tougher for Mom to understand what was being said. That morning in church, as the congregation burst into laughter, Mom sat in silence, missing out on the joke. It broke my heart, knowing how hard that was for her. Around that time Mom stopped going to church.

Her world was getting smaller.

Just before Christmas 2013, Mom lost the vision in her right eye. Despite immediate treatment, it never returned. Thankfully, her left eye did not give out, but Mom worried that it would go too, plunging her into darkness. The lack of vision in Mom's right eye robbed her of depth perception and I'm not certain, but I think that contributed to a further deterioration in her balance. For whatever reason, not long after her 90th birthday, Mom stopped being able to walk any distance at all, even with the Harley. By the summer of 2014, she was barely able to propel herself to the end of her short corridor and back.

Mom slowly gave up the activities that kept her mind, body and spirit going—church, daily stretch 'n flex, tai chi (done sitting down at TCG, so we called it tai chair), cranium crunchers, movies, happy hour, the "horse races," and a host of other activities she enjoyed.

The effort involved in attending these events was increasing, while the benefits were decreasing. As Mom's hearing and balance worsened and her trademark stamina declined, she was less and less able to participate. Even dressing and going to the dining room lost its appeal; Mom could no longer converse with her dinner mates who, themselves, were frequently hard of hearing.

Her world continued to shrink.

Thankfully, Mom got a captioned telephone, which made talking with her by phone possible. After her 90th birthday, more and more of our telephone conversations centered on her desire to "close this last chapter of my wonderful life." She felt useless, the greatest sin in her mind.

"If you took me down to the dining room," she asked during one of my visits, "Do you think that I could help fold the napkins?"

Mom desperately wanted to be productive, and didn't understand why she was still on this earth if she couldn't be.

"Every night I pray that God will take me, but he doesn't," she lamented. "I guess that's because I still have work to do here—but I don't know what it is because I'm not doing anything."

During one especially difficult conversation, Mom explained that she felt like a "big zero" and that the thought of continuing this "nothingness" for years and years was "almost more than I can bear." Hearing this from my sunny-side-up, silver-lining, glass-half-full mother, who had always put her best foot forward and seized the day, no matter what, was almost more than I could bear.

Mom often alluded to being put out on an "ice floe," referring to the Eskimo custom of setting elders adrift when they are no longer able to contribute to the tribe. Mom was much more afraid of living than dying, now that she felt she could no longer participate in life in a meaningful way.

Before my husband, Kevin, died of cancer in 2012, he embraced the theory that life is to be enjoyed, not endured. Mom was enduring, not enjoying, and she was ready to go. For Mom, her diminished, unproductive life was a fate worse than death.

"There needs to be a better system," Mom proclaimed.

As she had with Jack, Mom believed that her continued existence was a lose–lose situation; she was unhappy and felt that the time and resources going to care for her could be put to better use. Mom "wracked her brains" to come up with a better way to approach this end-of-life quandary, but was stymied. Never one to take "no" for an answer, it frustrated Mom that she couldn't single-handedly solve this dilemma.

"Okay, kids," Mom announced. "It's up to you to figure this out."

This became Mom's last crusade and, although I don't pretend to have any answers, a major impetus for writing this is to keep the dialog alive.[1]

As it became increasingly difficult for Mom to get dressed, make breakfast and otherwise perform those activities of daily living that doctors talk about, Mom's world shrank even more. She rarely left the Mouse House and she was lonely. For some time we had tried to convince Mom that she needed a companion; someone to chat with, who could help with meals and grooming; someone she could talk to. "A fake friend," she scoffed, dismissing the concept for the "umpteenth" time, as she would say. Mom's reticence was frustrating—she loved people. Mom knew where all the kids who worked in the dining room were from and delighted in talking to them about their native countries.

Eventually we decided that we could no longer take no for an answer and lined up someone to be with Mom a few hours a day, a few days a week. As expected, Mom and her Ukrainian helper, Luyba, hit it off immediately and Mom boasted that she was learning Russian.

Still, when we tried to increase the frequency of these visits, Mom resisted.

"I can't possibly be ready by 9 o'clock every morning," she explained.

So that was it; my snazzy, classy mother felt she had to be up and dressed, with her make-up on and best foot forward, before her "company" arrived!

---

1   In the process of writing this book I have discovered that there are several organizations dedicated to 'figuring out a better system'. See footnote 8.

Nevertheless, as Mom continued to decline, we increased the hours that Mom's helper was with her. The climbing cost of these services prompted us to explore other resources, including hospice. Jack and Kevin had both benefitted from hospice at the end of their lives.

A few months earlier, Mom had been diagnosed with myelodysplastic syndrome (MDS), a blood disease that eventually develops into leukemia. This terminal illness qualified Mom for hospice care—if she was willing to stop the Procrit/ transfusion regime that had been replenishing cells that her body was not producing on its own anymore. Hospice focuses on pain management and quality of life, rather than on curing patients. In order to qualify for its services, Mom had to have a terminal illness (being 90 years old does not count) and had to stop receiving treatment for that illness.

In July 2014, after discussions with the family and her doctors, Mom signed on with Avow Hospice. True to form, Mom carefully weighed the pros and cons before making this decision, but it didn't take her long. She was more than ready to "close this chapter," and here was a program designed to help achieve that goal. In hindsight, the MDS diagnosis was a true blessing—an answer to her prayers, Mom would have said—because it allowed her to take some control of this last phase of her life after all. When Mom asked how I felt about her hospice decision, I tried to be as honest as possible; I told her that, as hard as it was for me to imagine a world without her in it, it was harder still to think about her remaining in a world where she was so clearly unhappy.

In addition to the medical staff, hospice had a chaplain, a masseuse and a stream of volunteers who would read to Mom or spend a few hours with her when her regular care giver was unavailable. Services were provided in the Mouse House, and a nurse was available by telephone around the clock to answer questions or to come by, if needed. A volunteer even polished Mom's nails—the first time someone else had given her a manicure, Mom told me later. I appreciated hospice's practical approach: when getting Mom in and out of bed became a struggle, for instance, they brought in a hospital bed that made this much easier. When the trip from the bed to the toilet got to be a challenge, hospice arranged for a portable potty that sat right next to her bed.

Involving hospice did not alleviate the need for a caregiver, but it offered great additional support to Mom and the family. She was briefly taken for evaluation at the "Hospice House." While there, she received a catheter to cut down on her need to get out of bed to use the toilet, because Mom had started falling at night when she tried to get up. Thankfully, there wasn't far to fall and she never really hurt herself. The bigger problem was that she lacked the strength to get back into bed on her own and had to press what she called her "panic button" to summon one of the TCG aides to help.

By this point, we had increased Mom's private duty care services to 12 hours a day, seven days a week. Mom had become even less mobile and her Ukrainian helper had been replaced by younger, stronger women who Mom adored—and vice versa. Brenia was with Mom Monday through Friday and Tracey covered the weekend shift. But there were still 12 hours, from 8 p.m. until 8 a.m., when Mom was alone.

We pleaded with Mom countless times to use her "panic button" to call for assistance beforehand if she needed to get up at night. Mom would agree, and then fall again the next night. (Maddeningly, there are some regulations that prohibit bed restraints in places like TCG. Bed alarms, designed to beep loudly when the patient begins to get out of bed, are also taboo). The nurses surmised that Mom would simply forget that she couldn't walk when she'd wake up and need to use the bathroom. This was one of our first inklings that her mind was starting to go.

Here's another: Once Mom entered hospice, family members came to see her for a final time.

"I know why everyone is coming now," she proclaimed, in a "gotcha" tone.

"Because they love you," I answered. This conversation took place by telephone, but I didn't need to see her face to know that she was scoffing at my spin on the situation.

At that point, Mom seemed as sharp as ever, but not long thereafter, when some family members were in town for a visit, she asked, "Do you know what time their train leaves?…Do you think they will have time to stop here on their way to the station?"

There was no train service to Naples in all the time Mom lived there; Mom herself seemed to be traveling back in time. I told Mom that I didn't know their plans, rather than engaging in a conversation that might confuse her. This was to be the first of many such exchanges.

While visiting in October, I got a firsthand sense of how confused she could be at some times, while being totally lucid at others. We had spent several days together and, although Mom was more fatigued and less mobile than ever, her mental faculties seemed to be fully intact. The morning I was flying home, I stopped by the Mouse House early on my way to the airport. Mom had fallen the night before and I was determined to lecture her once again about not getting out of bed on her own. (I've heard that insanity is doing the same thing over and over, expecting different results; as I write these words, I see how insane this behavior was— and we were worried about *Mom's* mental state!)

Mom was still in bed when I arrived— or back in bed, I guess I should say. It was around 7:30 a.m. We had the "do not get out of bed without help" conversation and, although I don't recall it specifically, I am sure it went like all the others. I told Mom I couldn't stay long, reminding her that I was heading home and had a plane to catch. Mom studied her watch and then the wall clock. She questioned me about what time my flight was, how long the drive to the airport would take, and how far in advance I needed to be there. She studied her clock and watch some more, and suddenly became very animated.

Throwing off the covers, Mom inched her legs toward the edge of the bed, announcing, "I can be ready in five minutes."

We had a few difficult rounds, with me trying to explain to Mom why she couldn't go with me, and Mom pleading with me to let her come along. Finally, I had a brainstorm.

"You need to stay here and take care of Tiva," I told her.

That did the trick.

Little did I know at the time that, very shortly, I would have many more opportunities to convince my increasingly confused mother to stay in bed. Given her life on the go, it's no surprise that this was a hard sell.

I almost didn't get on the plane. Mom clearly needed around-the-clock supervision, but costs were skyrocketing. We were determined to keep Mom in the Mouse House, if at all possible, but this was becoming financially daunting. We would soon have to make some tough decisions. I did fly home that day, after arranging for a temporary nighttime aide, but I was distracted and consumed by Mom's situation. After talking it through with family members and friends, it became clear that I needed to return to Florida, both to alleviate some of the financial strain and to be with Mom during her last days.

At first, I thought that I would take over the day shift, since that would optimize time with Mom while she was awake. I quickly came to my senses. The heavy lifting—and I mean that literally as well as figuratively—happened during the day: feeding, bathing, dressing, changing. Brenia, Tracey and the hospice nurses and aides were far more able than I in these departments. So I became the night shift.

I'd never bought a one-way ticket, never left home and work without a firm return date. It was a strange concept; I told myself that it would only be a few weeks—Mom would live another week or two, then I would help finalize things and be back home by Thanksgiving. In retrospect, I had no clue but I guess I needed some kind of mental time frame to ground me.

I was uncertain how I was going to explain my return visit to Mom. Despite our frank conversations about her death, I didn't know how to tell her that I planned to stay with her until she died. Mom had always kept careful track of our arrival and departure dates on her calendar; should I just make up a date and then extend it, if need be?

By the time I returned to the Mouse House, less than a week after my last visit, this wasn't an issue. Mom didn't seem to find it unusual that I was back so soon, or ask how long I was going to stay.

Once in a while during the month I was with her, Mom would say, "So, you leave tomorrow?" and I would tell her that, no, I would be staying with her tomorrow. This seemed to comfort her. It did me.

And so, in late October 2014, I moved into the Mouse House. Lance and Lynn kindly provided a blow-up mattress that I put next to Mom's bed, arranging it so that my head was by the foot of her bed; that way we could face each other and I figured I would be in a better position to thwart any nighttime escapades.

A few days into the night shift, I began writing email updates each morning to keep the family abreast of what was going on with Mom. Because those reports could be somewhat grim (another "Mom word"), I started interspersing them with photos, clippings and stories that I found in Mom's treasure trove of files accumulated during her amazing around-the- world adventures. As Mom faded away from us in the bedroom, we kept her essence alive in the living room, as we shared her anecdotes, pictures and other tidbits from a full, richly-lived life. This balancing out of her final days with snippets from her earlier ones seemed to be a fitting tribute and I so enjoyed sharing both with my family.

Cindy, Mom and Jack celebrating Mom's 75th birthday in Captiva during
another week-long birthday celebration with the family, April 1999

I cannot overstate the group effort that went into caring for Mom and
Jack; over the years, the Fearsome Foursome and their Spectacular
Spouses contributed in every conceivable way to ensure Mom and
Jack's well-being. We each believed that the others' efforts were
more significant than our own. To borrow another of Mom's lines,
I thank my lucky stars to be part of such an amazing family, whose
love and support carried me through what turned out to be the most
extraordinary month of my life.

Here they are, my messages from the Mouse House:

Mouse House Night Shift
Checking In—November 1, 2014

Mom was wide awake before five this morning. First, she wanted to know how we were going to get the pictures glued to the wall next to her bed down. Next, Mom asked me about what we were going to do with the things in the drawers, and did we have a ladder to take down the picture over the bathroom door. At first I thought she was thinking about what would happen to her things after she died, but from her comments, I realized she was thinking that she, Tiva and I were all going somewhere. I didn't ask where, but I am sure the answer would have been "home." I didn't want to upset or confuse her by telling her she *was* home.

Mom was more animated and talkative than I've seen since my return. She asked if the car was packed, and then said, "Wait, we don't have a car."

She looked confused. She asked me to get Tiva's carrier from Lance's garage, and that's when I told her we weren't going anywhere right now. I told her that I was going to stay with Tiva and her. She fell back to sleep about then, but I don't think I have heard the last of this conversation.

That's the latest from here. Mom has been pretty much eating in bed and sleeping, and that's it. I had a long talk with Jennifer, the Avow Hospice nurse, yesterday. No update on when "the end" may come... but the deterioration is marked since my last visit less than two weeks ago. Jennifer told me emphatically that I shouldn't tell family members that I would "tell them when the time comes," as this can be extremely hard to gauge—sometimes family comes and the loved one hangs on longer than expected, sometimes they go so quickly there is no warning. So... I will do my best, with that caveat.

On a cheerier note, happy birthday Sharon! And happy November to all.

xxoo C

Greetings from the Mouse House— November 2, 2014

Good Morning and Welcome to Daylight Savings Time!

Highlights from yesterday: Mom seemed to fluctuate between thinking we were moving somewhere else, and (mentally) rearranging the Mouse House to accommodate company. She asked me to move several photos off one of the end tables in the living room so that it would be "easier for people to put their drinks down." This is a table she looks at all day from her bed.

Speaking of bed… Although Brenia told me she'd had Mom outside for an hour or so the day before I arrived (which would have been last Monday), I don't think she's been out of bed since I got here, other than to use the bathroom—and those visits are much less frequent because of the catheter. She was funny yesterday, asking about where the new bed came from, telling me how small it was and saying she wouldn't want a bed like that "most of the time." I told her I thought that it was good for now and she seemed to be okay with that. (For those who don't know, the hospital bed was provided by hospice and the ability to raise and lower it—and Mom—makes life a lot easier).

In a similar vein, the other day we were brushing Mom's teeth using one of those moon-shaped plastic jobs that they have in hospitals when you don't have a sink. She asked me if I used one of them at home, and I said no.

"Neither do I," says she…

Throughout the day yesterday, out of the blue, Mom asked me to locate certain seemingly random items. She couldn't really explain why she needed me to find these things—it seemed to me that she was making sure they wouldn't be forgotten in the "move."

At one point, Mom asked where Kirk was, as though she'd just realized he wasn't in the room. Later, she started talking about the various houses she'd lived in, saying she guessed she liked contemporaries the best, like the one Alicia and _____ lived in. She struggled but could not come up with Scott's name—sorry bro. I even prompted her with "the most beautiful baby boy ever." She nodded, but the name just wasn't there…

Mom did look at her newspaper in bed a bit, even turning a page. (During recent visits the newspapers have piled up in a way they never used to, but we are forbidden from tossing them out, at least until she's perused them.)

Anyway, Mom ate very little yesterday, mostly dessert. Jennifer says not to push her to eat—she says that we tend to associate feeding with love, but it's a mistake to force food on Mom if she doesn't want it.

I guess that these are the highlights. I am so glad that I am here, it seems to comfort Mom—at least I know it comforts me. She has said to me, "You are a sight for sore eyes" and "Just looking at you makes me feel better."

I try to sit next to her bed and read or work some during the day so that, when she wakes up, she can see that I am there.

I am sorry if these updates are too long. I think it's good for me to write this stuff down.

I love you all and am so glad that we are in this together.

xxoo Your Favorite Sister

A QUIET DAY AT THE MOUSE HOUSE—NOVEMBER 3, 2014

Greetings All,

Mom is sleeping more and more. When she was awake yesterday it was for very brief moments. She ate very little, although she did scarf down a donut I brought up from a function downstairs. She seems to favor the things she can pick up with her hands—mostly sweets.

The only thing close to a conversation that we had yesterday was when I had returned back to the Mouse House around 10 a.m. after going to Lance and Lynn's house to take care of Saba (their dog) and their other critters, while they are out of town.

"You're back!" Mom beamed.

I'm pretty sure that she thought I'd just come in from the Virgin Islands, despite the fact that we'd said good morning to each other only an hour or so before. I tried to get a clear answer from her about this, but she was confused and I didn't push it.

Not to put too fine a point on it, but Mom didn't get out of bed at all yesterday or the day before. Her bottom is now quite red and Nurse Sophia suggested that we turn her every two hours from side to side, to alleviate what I guess are bed sores. Poor Mom—her bowels go from overzealous to shut down. There are some medical issues that

5

seemingly need to be addressed—I won't go into detail here, but call me if you'd like to get the nitty-gritty.

Mom received two packages in the mail yesterday—a note and pictures from Jessica from Belle and Co.'s recent visit to the Mouse House; and a note and brochures from Becca, including the announcement of her engagement to Jason! Sadly, Mom was not with it enough yesterday to see either one—I am hoping that she is up to it today. She also received the monthly check from the VA. I am unsure whether she'll be able to endorse it; if not I will deposit it and hope for the best.

"I can't write anymore," she told me the other day.

I recently came upon a note Mom wrote after her 90th birthday, with her classic penmanship that we'd all know anywhere. Now, even the circles around her menu choices are shaky scribbles.

From a pamphlet called "When the Time Comes"[2] provided the other day by Nurse Jennifer:

> People near the end of life will sometimes talk about travel, as though they are planning a journey... This type of conversation is referred to as symbolic language, and may be one of the ways people let us know that they are preparing for death or are trying to tell us goodbye.

Another passage that caught my eye:

> You don't have to do or say anything to make things better. Just be there as fully as you can.[3]

---

2   Published by Quality of Life Publishing Company and copyright by Hospice of Santa Cruz County; reprinted with permission.

3   Passage written by Sogyal Rinpoche.

I guess that's about it from here. I am working with TCG and hospice to tweak medicines, etc., but I don't think everyone needs the skinny on that. FYI, Aunt Jo and Uncle Charley and Jessica have asked to be, and have been, included on these updates—so mind your manners when replying—G1 and G3 (okay, 2½) are listening![4]

Love to all, C.

PS: Today would have been Kevin's 65th birthday.

---

4   G1 is Mom's generation, G2 is mine, G3 is the nieces… but since Jess is the eldest we call her G2 ½.

RESTLESS TIMES AT THE MOUSE HOUSE—NOVEMBER 4, 2014

Good Morning All,

Yesterday morning I almost wrote a follow-up to my morning note, because Mom woke up early and was chatty and pretty coherent. She asked about Saba (who'd been sick the day before) and wanted me to turn on her fiber optic pumpkin, which made her smile. Her voice is very soft now, barely a whisper. She asked if I was leaving tomorrow and I said, "No." That was the end of that conversation.

Mom probably ate more at breakfast than she had the entire previous day. While she was eating her breakfast—an extremely laborious process—a gal came from hospice to help her bathe. She and Brenia determined that Mom was too weak to get into the shower, so they gave her a sponge bath in bed. This resulted in having to manually move Mom around quite a bit, and she moaned and groaned throughout the process.

Mom fell asleep around 11:00 and slept for the rest of the day. She didn't eat any lunch or dinner and only had a few sips of water when we put the straw to her lips. She was sleeping more soundly than she has been during the day. She briefly opened her eyes and smiled at Lance when he arrived here in the late afternoon and then went right back to sleep.

Two of her apparently classic "end of life" symptoms are restlessness and anxiety. Mom was agitated some of the other nights I've been here, but last night was by far the worst. She tossed, turned, pulled at her nightie, and moaned loudly. She was mostly asleep, but a couple of times asked me, "What's the matter?"

Yesterday, Nurse Jennifer taught me a trick about giving Mom the anxiety medicine in a syringe by diluting the pill in a few drops of water, so I did that and gave it to her. Although it had some effect, I am going to have to ask about having the dosage increased, because Mom continued to carry on for several more hours. At about 2:30 this morning I tried to give her some morphine to help ease her restlessness. It is administered through a syringe under her tongue, and although Mom had allowed me to do that with the Ativan hours earlier, she clenched her jaw and would not open her mouth to let me give her the medicine.

"What you are doing? Please, no!" she begged, with a very scared look in her eye, as if I was coming at her with a sharp instrument.

I will have to talk to Jennifer about this issue, too.

Mom finally fell into a good sleep around 3:30 a.m., I guess, and is still sound asleep as I write. It was a tough night.

During Jennifer's visit yesterday, she noted some physical changes—including darkened urine, indicating that the dying process may be accelerating. Jennifer will visit Mom daily now, to keep a closer eye on her. Jennifer told Lance and me how impressed she was with our family, and how wonderful it was for Mom to have such a loving, supportive group. It was quite nice to hear. Of course Mom gets full credit. How I wish she could hear these sentiments (or "sediments," as she would surely quip).

That's it for now. Mom seems to be stirring and is agitated again, poor thing. I love you all,

C

MANNERS MATTER AT THE MOUSE HOUSE—NOVEMBER 5, 2014

I am pleased to report that, after a couple of rough days and nights with Mom being very agitated—moaning loudly and thrashing around — I think we've discovered that, ironically, this was a negative reaction to her anxiety medicine. She's been sleeping comfortably since around midnight, thank goodness. Even in her most agitated state, when I could hear a few coherent words, they were often "I beg your pardon," or "pretty please could you help me?" Despite everything, Mom's manners remain impeccable.

I am sure that these awful episodes have taken a lot out of Mom and I hope that she continues to sleep comfortably. She did seem to know Lance and Lynn when they were here yesterday and, in a few semi-coherent moments, asked about Dana and Carly. Mostly, what she says is either unintelligible or out of context—except to her, of course.

Mom's still packing and moving—she told me yesterday to remember the brown suitcase. She and Jack have had matching red suitcases for many years. I envision the brown suitcase she's referring to as a big, clunky one from the Stone Lodge attic going back many moons, long before suitcases had wheels.

Mom's concern for others at this point is amazing. One of the clearest thoughts she had yesterday was when Brenia was trying to feed her and Mom asked,

"Has your husband had his dinner yet?"

Speaking of food, Mom eats very little now, and can't really feed herself anymore.

That's about it from here today. Many thanks and love to you all.

Xxoo

GREEN FLASHES AND GOOMBAY
SMASHES—NOVEMBER 6, 2014

Good Morning All,

No, I haven't bailed and gone to Fiji, nor have I lost my senses! But I have spent the last few evenings sorting through many, many, *many* AKS files, filled with photos, clippings, pieces of her autobiography, notes and maps… and Green Flashes and Goombay Smashes were the names of two back-to back-files that made me smile. There's a poem (or a Jimmy Buffet song) in there somewhere; stay tuned.

This file review exercise is a wonderful way to stay connected to the essence of Mom, while she fades away physically. I can see her now, mixing up a batch of her famous Goombay Smashes and heading to the Gulf for sunset and the prospect of that elusive green flash…

Mom really hasn't awakened since the night before last, when we finally got her calmed down. Brenia and I tried to waken her several times yesterday to feed her, with no success. Other than one sip of water in the morning, she had nothing to eat or drink yesterday and little if anything is passing through her. The great news is that Mom appears to be resting comfortably. Brenia (with my feeble assistance) gave Mom a sponge bath and changed her nightie last evening. Except for a slight groan when we must have hurt her bad shoulder, Mom was unresponsive. As sad as this is, it is so much better than her agitated state. If I had to guess, I would say that she's spoken her last words in this life. Now it's just a matter of her systems shutting down—and who knows how long that could take?

I am so glad that I am here with her. The exercise of going through Mom's files makes the time especially poignant. I don't mean to tell anyone reading this how to grieve... but I encourage everyone to think not just about who we are losing, but also who we have had all of these years. Mom is so alive in all of us—even little Belle; Mom loved this photo of Belle looking up at the world globe during Belle's recent visit to the Mouse House. I'm saving the files that I think will be of interest to G2 and G3, for us to sort through at Christmastime.

I don't know what else to say right now. I guess this is a little heavy for you all to be reading as you begin your day. Mom would encourage us all to *carpe diem*. I think I will focus on that today.

Love to all, C

OUT OF THE BLUE—NOVEMBER 7, 2014

Happy Friday to All,

Thanks to all for your calls, emails, chats and visits. I feel so fortunate to have this wonderful family to help me through this transition.

My guess that Mom had spoken her last words the other day was wrong... She was a tiny bit more alert yesterday than she'd been the day before. She ate a little applesauce and some of Lance's special homemade tapioca and had a few sips of water. Lance and Lynn came by and she greeted them with one of her smiles that lights up the room, even now.

Mom's still moving, or perhaps I should say WE are still moving. Yesterday Mom asked me, out of the blue,

"Who is going to drive us?"

I told her I didn't know yet and she closed her eyes again.

At one point I put Tiva on the bed where she could pet him.

"Isn't he a nice doggy," she said, smiling.

Another time, I was wearing one of her tops. She opened her eyes and said,

"That looks good on you."

Always an eye for fashion!

She didn't say much more than that yesterday and the couple of times that she asked me something, she had dozed off before I had time to write the answer on the white board.

We had a brief episode of awful arthritis pain but, thankfully, got that under control and Mom slept comfortably all night. The hospice nurse was here to check on her and noted some changes that indicate further decline, although she was still unable to say when the end might be, other than "days or weeks" (down from "weeks or months" not very long ago). The nurse did say that the tougher people are, the longer they tend to hold on—to which Lance quipped, "Oh God, let's start choosing her Easter basket."

The file sorting has been such fun. Yesterday, I found the list of Christmas cards Mom and Dad received in 1956, and an adorable hand drawn koala Christmas card from our family when we lived in Australia, "designed by Scott and Lance." I also found Mom's original drawing of the Holly Springs School, for which she won a prize when she was in the 4th grade. Another file contained three original newspaper clippings announcing the Herber/Kuntz wedding in the wonderful year of 1957. It goes on and on—and when you think about how many miles this stuff has travelled… Amazing!

What else? I am concerned about Tiva this morning; he is being very quiet, not his normal pesky self. He clearly senses that something is wrong. He has become very protective of Mom and meows his head off at the nurses when they touch her. Everyone predicts that he won't last long once Mom is gone and I truly believe that, especially after seeing what happened to our dog Hoot after Kevin died. I must say that Tiva has served a vital role in the life and well-being of Mom (and Jack) for the last 15-plus years and has certainly earned his wings.

I guess that's it for the morning report. Much love to all, and thanks for sharing the journey. I can't imagine doing this without you all.

xxoo C

A Few of Her Favorite Things—November 8, 2014

Good Morning from the Mouse House,

Mom was awake early, so I was able to feed her a few bites of cream of wheat and to sneak her pills into her (ground up with a bit of chocolate ice cream; works like a charm). I've learned all kinds of nifty nursing tips lately—but believe me I am not quitting my day job!

Mom has been a bit more restless over the past few days, which is to be expected near the end per hospice and its literature. She's not really speaking much anymore, although when I showed her a picture of Stone Lodge with pretty fall leaves, she said, "Look at those mountains!"

Mom used to tell me that as a little girl she loved lying in her bed and looking at the mountains through her bedroom window.

Mom's parents who we called Gramp and Grandma, in front of Stone Lodge, in Hunters Run, Pennsylvania where Mom grew up (Photo taken by Lance)

The file excavation continues to be a great way of remembering Mom's adventurous spirit. There are files upon files of maps, travel brochures, trip itineraries, DO NOT DISTURB signs from hotels around the world, and a page cut out of a travel magazine listing how to say "hello," "good bye," "please" and "thank you" in Arabic, French, German, Greek, Italian, Japanese, Mandarin, Portuguese, Russian, Spanish, Swahili and Swedish!

Also—a real bonus—a list that Mom wrote on July 4th of this year, which she titled:

Favorite Things: (As far as I know, she did this without prompting)

```
Moons
Convertibles
Blue
Snorkeling
Sax
Sunsets
Cats
Lobster
```

Not a bad list...

I've been thinking about her list of *not* so favorite things:

```
People chewing gum
Plaids and stripes together
Showing bra straps
Misplaced apostrophe's  ;-)
```

Busy this a.m. as Mom is awake and fidgety.

Love to all xxoo

PS: Tiva back to his pesky self

WHAT A WONDERFUL WORLD— NOVEMBER 9, 2014

Good Morning All,

Yesterday Mom was more awake than she's been in days—perhaps the "surge of energy" when the end is near, as described in the Avow pamphlet and predicted by Nurse Jennifer. Mom was a bit restless, clearly wanting to get out of bed and asking over and over what the schedule was. I am projecting, but it's hard to imagine not having an agenda after a lifetime of appointments, commitments and deadlines (even if it's only getting to the dining room before it closes).

Mom's questions were still mostly incoherent, but she gave Tracey a big smile and "Good morning!" when she arrived and was happy to see Lance and Lynn, too (Lance got a big "You're back!" every time he entered Mom's room). Mom groaned when Lance and I broke into song and teased Tracey by pulling on her locks as if ringing a bell. Last night, as Tracey was leaving, Mom said to both of us, "Good night, you go to sleep now, and don't forget to close your eyes."

In describing Mom's recent energy surge to Jaclynn yesterday, Jaclynn said that when her Mom had worked with terminal patients, the caregivers described this as the stage when the previously sedate patients would suddenly perk up and be alert, "as if they hadn't gotten the memo."

From the great finds in the files department, I bring you today's pearl from the Life and Times of AKS: a list written by Mom last year on Thanksgiving (again, unprompted, as far as I know):

Fine family taking winter trips to Clearwater, Florida, 1927-1938.

High school and college adventures—editing both weekly newspapers, etc., etc.

Interesting career with army information school as editor-in-chief.

Side kick Harvard B. School.

Three fabulous children and Kirk, too.

[Sorry, just making sure you are paying attention!]

Two terrific romances, 25 years and 37 years.

Living overseas 1963-66, travel around the world, and around and around.

Unbelievable friends

Animals to love

Boats and more boats

Finally, magnificent Moonglow, live aboard 3 years

Is that all there is?

SEIZE THE DAY!

[Emphasis in the original, as we say in my biz.]

That's it from here today. Cue Louis Armstrong's "What a Wonderful World." I love you all.

xxoo C

P.S. Kevin died 2 years ago today...

WHERE ARE WE GOING NEXT?—NOVEMBER 10, 2014

Good Morning All,

Yesterday was kind of a mixed bag: at times Mom was very lucid, and at other times pretty out of it. When she noticed that I was wearing one of her tops, Mom said very clearly to Lynn and Tracey,

"Cindy and I have worn the same size for years."

And when looking at the adorable picture of Belle pointing to the world globe, she said,

"That child is wearing high heels."

Yes, there is definitely a theme.

Mom also asked Tracey what material her leggings were made from. She may be fading fast, but Mom has not lost her sense of fashion. That makes one of us; not that I had one to lose.

On the other hand, Mom asked me several times where we were yesterday. When I told her we were at TCG, she said,

"Virginia?"

I finally got it across that we were in the Mouse House. Her follow-up question was,

"So where are we going next?"

I told her it was cold and rainy outside and we were going to stay in for now. She seems to be embracing the last advice she gave to Kevin—"Always plan one more destination."

At one point, after persisting as only she can about wanting to get out of bed, Tracey and I moved Mom one step, from her bed to the portable commode. Moving was excruciatingly hard on her, in both directions. Mom had a few bites of tapioca, apple sauce and some Ensure yesterday. I tried to feed her a few bites of omelet last evening, but she couldn't even swallow that.

In the category of a picture says 1000 words, the goody from the files today is a photo taken by Kirk on Mom's 80th birthday in the Abacos. Those of you who are on the ball will remember that snorkeling was on her list of favorite things…

Do something special, spontaneous and adventurous today, and think of AKS. Love to all, xxoo

NEVER A DULL MOMENT AT THE MOUSE HOUSE!—NOVEMBER 11, 2014

Good Morning Campers,

Mom was awake pretty much all day yesterday and seemed to be a bit more "present," at least some of the time. She had a passel of company: an aide, RN, social worker and chaplain, all from hospice; a couple of the TCG gals who come by to say "hi," even though they aren't assigned to her anymore; Fay, Lance, Lynn.

Mom surprised me—although she didn't interact much with her visitors, after one of the nurses left, Mom whispered,

"She's the one I'm so fond of."

Lynn stopped by while I was out and Mom was very taken with her outfit (back to fashion...) and asked Lynn where I was (I'd run to the store). Although brief, Mom did have a few of these "normal" conversations yesterday—more so than I recall in several days. Nevertheless, Fay, who hadn't seen Mom for five days, said that she noticed a real decline.

Perhaps it was prompted by all the visitors, but while Lynn was here, Mom started talking in a way that made it clear that she thought we were going to have a party in the Mouse House. I guess Mom figured if I wouldn't let her go anywhere, she'd bring the action to her. Mom was worried about where everyone would sit, tried to explain to me where the candlesticks are (none in the Mouse House) and asked,

"Will there be a bartender, or not?"

Later, she asked why everyone was taking so long to get here.

Just when I think that Mom's "not in there" anymore, she shows me that that's not the case. That said, these moments are fleeting and there are plenty of times that she falls asleep mid-sentence or talks nonsensically. Like a child who can't speak but can comprehend some, she seems to struggle to get her point across and then gives up because the effort wears her out. She's so sweet—she speaks very softly most of the time and, when I don't hear her, I put my ear down close to her mouth so she can repeat what she said... and she just kisses me, instead! I guess part of what I am trying to explain is that Mom's mind is all over the place now and she can't really focus for very long at all (with the possible exception of party planning and fashion).

You may recall that Mom's mind jumped around in the best of times. It was a joke with Jack.

Out of the blue, Mom would say to Jack, "Do you remember that little place we had tea?"

And Jack would say, "Category, Doll: Continent? Decade? Give me some frame of reference."

It's that same mind that is now hopping all over the world and the last nine decades and I never know when or where it's going to alight.

I keep forgetting to report how universally Mom is loved by her caregivers—the private duty gals, the hospice folks, the TCG staff—EVERYONE remarks on how sweet, polite and friendly she is. I don't think it's just lip service and, of course, I believe it to be true as well. Brenia went so far as to say that Mom was the first nice person she's ever worked for.

"Damned with faint praise," I'm sure Mom would reply.

And the tidbit of the day from the Amazing AKS Archives is a newspaper clipping (undated) announcing John Chancellor's appointment as director of the Voice of America, with a 1947 photo taken at the Carlisle Barracks, picturing Chancellor, AKS and some other folks. Mom is described under the photo as "Mrs. Donald Shearer, then editor of the Carlisle Barracks newspaper for which Chancellor was a reporter. (Chancellor went on to become anchor of NBC News.)

So there it is. Enjoy your day. Thanks for listening. Mom, Tiva and I send our love from the Mouse House to each of you.

xxoo, C

Ahoy from M/V Mouse House—November 12, 2014

Good Morning to All,

First thing yesterday morning, Mom asked, "Where's my black bag?" referring, I was sure, to her pocketbook that has been like her right arm all these years—but which she obviously hasn't needed recently. Poor thing, she probably worried about that all night—a gal needs her pocketbook no matter what age she is or what continent she's on. I pointed to the dresser and told her that her bag was in a drawer. I could tell that she either didn't understand or didn't buy it, so I went to the drawer, took out the pocketbook and handed it to her.

She looked confused at first, but then she lit up and asked,

"Where are we going?"

I think she set me up, don't you?

This kind of exchange happens all the time; by the time I can write an answer to her question on the white board, she's forgotten the question and looks at me like I'm crazy (as in, "Why are you writing nonsense to me?").

In my ongoing attempt to try to explain Mom's current mental state, here's a snapshot:

From her bed yesterday afternoon, Mom could see that a lamp was on in the living room.

"Why is that lamp on now, we don't need that light," she said, correctly (bringing to mind Grandma's comment under such circumstances, that the light was "burning a hole in the day").

Anyway, Mom's noticing, and concern for, the unnecessary light indicated to me a totally normal awareness and orientation. (Although, of course, it doesn't mean that she knew we were in the Mouse House.) Not very long thereafter, we had this exchange (with me writing on the white board):

MOM: What time is it? (Looking at her watch and the clock on the wall, but apparently not believing either of them).

ME: It's 4:30.

MOM: In the morning? (?? It's light, Brenia is with us in the room...)

ME: No, Mom, in the evening...

After a short pause:

MOM: Did you check overboard? (Pointing with her finger down over the side of the bed.)

ME: Yes, there's nothing there.

(I do my best to "go along" with these conversations, with mixed results; it sounds to me like we are on the water—reminiscent of when Jack was near the end and thought he was in a plane).

MOM: (After more discussion of the time) So, who's cooking dinner?

ME: The Chef.

MOM: Is he already on board?

Aha! So we are at sea...

As to the physical part: Mom is, as you've probably surmised, totally bed-ridden. With great effort and patience, Brenia and I (mostly Brenia) can get her from the bed to the commode right next to the bed. Mom is very afraid and groans loudly throughout the process, yet she has been more and more insistent about wanting to get up. I tell her, as I did this morning, that I can't get her up by myself, but that doesn't register. I called the nurse's station for help yesterday morning before Brenia arrived, but after an hour, no one had shown up... (yes, I reported the incident).

Anyway, it is excruciating not to be able to grant Mom her request and she becomes very agitated. Ugh. I count the minutes on the clock until Brenia will appear and apologize to Mom for not being able to help her. Not only am I physically unable to move her, I am horribly afraid of hurting her and, even though she doesn't understand, I tell myself it's for her own good. Guess parents go through that all the time, but boy is it tough!

Through it all, Mom seizes the day: we were bathing and changing her in bed yesterday, repeatedly rolling her from side to side, which she hates. However, at one point, when she rolled over on her side and could see out the window, she perked up and said,

"Look at that blue sky!"

On that note, here's the gem of the day, taken from Mom's "Adele Scrapbook" file. I'm unsure of the context—somehow associated with real estate, I am guessing. Typed on a single page, with a gold seal and ribbon at the bottom, is this short message (author unknown):

ADELE SCULLY

IF YOU NEED HELP TALKING PEOPLE INTO DOING THINGS, CALL ADELE. HER SPARKLING ENTHUSIASM MELTS ALL NEGATIVE THOUGHTS OR REPLIES.

There it is. Over and out from the good ship Mouse House. Look at the puffy white clouds in the blue sky, and think of Mom and her sparkling enthusiasm.

Love to all xxoo C

HAIL THE HULA HOOP QUEEN—
NOVEMBER 13, 2014

Good Morning All,

Mom slept virtually all day yesterday, eating very little and saying even less. I did get a couple of big bright smiles out of her. First thing in the morning when she saw me she smiled and said,

"You're so pretty."

(I can hear three brothers making wisecracks here: now it's clear that Mom is delusional! But I beat you to the punch and saved you the effort).

Although she groans when we move her—and sometimes without any provocation (especially at night)—Mom does not seem to be in a lot of pain. I usually give her a small dose of morphine once a day when she asks for it or seems especially restless, but the prescription allows it to be administered much more frequently. I am pleased that that hasn't been necessary up to this point.

The files continue to turn up amazing documents, including:

- the notes she made while job hunting in Cambridge when Dad was at "the B-School;"

- the wages paid to our nanny in Bedford Village;

- a note from Scott dated June 8, 1962, thanking Mom for coming with his class to Bear Mountain;

- a note from Kirk dated May 4, 1973, promising to do better at school and apologizing for yelling at Mom (this one *not* fabricated by me) and

- An original letter on Pan American Airways stationery addressed to Mr. and Mrs. Shearer apologizing for the half-hour delay in their flight's departure.

There is also a blue ribbon from the Pinellas County Fair dated 1936, with a note in Grandma's writing explaining that Mom won this prize for a scarf she made in Italian hemstitching class while at Clearwater Junior High School when she was 11 years old.

Of course, I could go on and on—these files are truly extraordinary. Instead, I will attach another photo with that amazing smile, taken on the back porch of Stone Lodge. For those of us who have seen Mom struggle with her balance for so long, it's hard to believe that at one point she was a hula hoop queen!

Several days ago when she was more with it, I showed Mom this photo and we had a good time talking about Stone Lodge and her memories of rolling a big steel hoop down the driveway with a stick, walking on stilts, and dressing the kittens in doll clothes, then pushing them around in a baby carriage.

Thanks to all for your kind words and thoughts. It makes this process so much easier to go through knowing that you are all here with us in spirit.

Love to all, C.

WHAT ARE WE WAITING FOR?—
NOVEMBER 14, 2014 (A.M.)

Good Morning from the MH Night Shift,

Mom was as awake and alert yesterday as she'd been sleepy and out of it the day before. For the most part, she was in good spirits. She even sat up in bed for a bit and read—or at least looked at—one of Lance's stories in the *Naples Daily News*. Interestingly, she even remembered to tell him that when he dropped by a short time later, though she also asked Lance if she'd seen him since he took her for observation at the Hospice House several weeks back. (Answer: yes; virtually every day).

I finally think I have a small sense of Mom's mental state right now. You know how sometimes in a dream there will be people, houses, etc., that converge in a way that's never happened in reality, but somehow in the dream it seems to make sense? I think of Mom's current awareness like that; in the same conversation, she told Lynn last evening that she'd been on a long trip and also told her she hadn't been out of bed for weeks. When we put in a call to Aunt Jo and Uncle Charley yesterday, Mom also reported to them that she/we had just returned from a big trip, although she couldn't recall where we'd been.

There are a couple of core threads that seem to run throughout Mom's thoughts. First, she is obsessed with time. For those of us who have been given the task of replacing her watch battery, we know that Mom is lost without her watch, so needing to know the time isn't a new phenomenon. However, she's taken this to a new level.

"That clock on the wall is wrong," she'll tell me, even though it has the same time as the wristwatch she's staring at on her oh-so-skinny arm. When Lance arrives, she asks what time *his* watch says, needing a third opinion.

She's constantly asking me what time it is and then challenging my response.

"*Two thirty?*" Mom repeats incredulously, as if that's preposterous.

A.M. and P.M. are confusing too.

"Why is it dark?" Mom asked last evening, hours after night had fallen, Brenia had gone and Mom's P.M. routine had been completed.

"Because it's nighttime," I told her—and she gave me one of her classic skeptical looks.

The other thread is home/travel.

"When are we going home?"

"How much longer till we get home?"

"*This* is home? Then why haven't I seen the animals?" (She phrases this last question like a "gotcha," so I rattle the cat treat tin to summon Tiva).

Mom is, understandably, very restless.

"What are we doing now?" she asks. And, more poignantly,

"What are we waiting for?"

I can almost hear her say, "Let's get this show on the road." Ever her mother's daughter, idleness is not Mom's strong suit.

The toughest for me, yesterday, was a new question. It started in the morning, and then I thought was forgotten, but it came up again last night. I hope I can type this without bawling...

"Where's Dada? I want Dada.... Why doesn't he come to my room?"

I told Mom he was sleeping. A little bit later, she asked me,

"Is Gramp sleeping?" and I said,

"Yes. You will see him soon."

Nothing more was said until she was falling asleep.

"I don't know why Gramp won't come to see me," she said sadly. (She called him Dada and we called him Gramp, so she used both terms.)

I told her he'd come to see her when she was sleeping, but she didn't understand and thought I had said *he* was sleeping.

"You always say that; he can't be sleeping *all* the time," she insisted.

Ugh. Perhaps if this comes up today, Gramp can be off on one of those long trips...

*Mom and Gramp in a grapefruit tree in 1928, when Gramp was
an itinerant fruit picker during their winters in Florida*

And now, from the archives, a snippet taken from the Carlisle High
School Graduation 1941 Program:

THE 1926 CUP

TO THAT STUDENT WHO SHALL HAVE CONTRIBUTED
MOST TO THE MORALE OF THE SCHOOL DURING
THE YEAR. FOR HIS OR HER CONTRIBUTION
TO THE SCHOOL LEADERSHIP: LOYALTY TO
SCHOOL AND FACULTY; SCHOLARSHIP AND
EXTRA CURRICULAR ACTIVITIES, PARTICULARLY
MUSIC, DRAMATICS AND PUBLICATIONS, THIS
CUP IS AWARDED TO ADELE KUNTZ.

No wonder she has a hard time being still! For extra credit, guess who won the 1926 Cup the following year?

Signing off from the Mouse House. Happy Friday, and love to all. Thanks for sharing the journey...

C

PARTY AT THE MOUSE HOUSE!—
NOVEMBER 14, 2014 (P.M.)

Greetings, All... (Like on-line newspapers, you are getting tomorrow's update tonight!)

Actually, I'm pretty sure tonight's party isn't really at the Mouse House, but I'm not certain where we are. I've been instructed to put the drinks on trays on the dining room table, to get "a million little napkins, do you have them? What do they look like?"... To make sure we have lots of ice and to put out candy in little dishes. Mom then says that she will take care of putting out the candy and starts (for the umpteenth time, in AKS lingo) to try to get up. I am fairly certain she thinks she can do this on her own without a problem. I tell her I will take care of the candy dishes later—but she's skeptical.

"We should put the candy dishes out now," she tells me.

"Okay," say I, heading out of the room.

She calls me back, mentioning water (ice water is her most frequent request). I lift her water glass and steer the straw toward her mouth. She's not interested.

"We need to put the water out in glasses on the table," she tells me.

Poor thing.

Interspersed with these requests are a million indecipherable mumblings that are clearly related to the party details.

No small wonder that this occupies her mind. Mom's files are full of party invitations from the Shearers and Scullys:

"Come for a Nip and a Nibble,"

"Bad Moon Rising Party–Hip Boots Optional,"

along with pages of typed lists on Colgate Palmolive stationery containing the names of guests for countless AKS/DKS gala affairs. Remember her story from a party in Manila when she'd instructed the kitchen staff to make sure there was an apple in the mouth when the roast pig was presented—and the maid serving the guests came in with the pig, but the apple was in *her* mouth?

Anyway, as if this party planning wasn't consuming enough, Mom's also been rearranging the furniture—and even the rooms here—wherever "here" is at the moment.

"This is home???" she asks once again, still incredulous.

I tell her "Yes" and that she named it "The Mouse House." Mom smiles, as if she thinks that's a cute name... but keeps pushing.

"What's in there, the dining room?" she asks, pointing at the bathroom.

"No, the bathroom," I tell her.

"So what's out there?"

And so on. I think we are going to turn the closet into the dining room. Lots about dining rooms and dining room tables today. At one point when she woke up, she said,

"I guess I shouldn't be up here on this table."

When I asked her why she was there, she explained she didn't know where else to be—but she knew she shouldn't be on the table.

Thankfully, no more talk about Gramp. Phew. I had his trip all figured out, just in case. Mom did, however, ask at some point today,

"What time is Grandma's program?" as she studied her watch.

"I don't know," I said, and that was the end of that.

Mom's best line of the day came first thing this morning. She'd already given me two or three big smiles and "Good morning, you're here!" greetings, every time she'd awake after dozing back off. Then Brenia arrived and got a number of big hellos as well.

After the third or fourth time Mom saw Brenia, Mom said to her,

"Boy, I've been seeing you everywhere I go!"

Mom has also started to mention seeing people who aren't here. So far I don't think it's anyone she can identify and the hospice folks did alert us to the possibility of this phenomenon. Stay tuned…

The gem of the day comes from two *Naples Daily News* articles from her AKS Scrapbook file.[5] The first is from 1978, when Mom was awarded the Associate of the Year Award by the Naples Area Board of Realtors. The accompanying article says that Mrs. Scully received double honors, as she was also installed as the President of the Women's Council for the coming year. In the second photo, Mom is presenting the Associate of the Year Award. Look at that smile!

Good night all. Happy weekend. Stay warm, and don't forget to smell the roses (or the pinecones)…

xxoo C

---

5   Reprinted with the permission of the *Naples Daily News*, where they were originally published.

GOOD MORNING FROM MOM AND ME (NOT MOM AND I) AT THE MOUSE HOUSE— NOVEMBER 16, 2014

Hi All,

I get my love of alliteration, persnicketiness about basic rules of grammar and about a bazillion-and-one other things from Mom. (Here she would say, "I've told you a million times not to exaggerate!") Although she is less and less able to verbalize a thought, I can hear Mom in my head, knowing what she would say in various circumstances. When I am here, with her, I keep myself distracted with busyness, but yesterday I took a break and wandered around a craft fair at Unity Church across the street. It's the kind of thing Mom and I would do together and I was struck by how present she was in my thoughts. I knew what she'd like and what she'd pooh-pooh. I missed her so much I could barely breathe.

Sorry, not sure where that came from. You're in luck; my report from yesterday is short...

Mom was very tired and said little; perhaps all the party planning caught up with her.

"Where is everyone?" she asked first thing yesterday morning.

Mom was able to sit up in her wheelchair with the doors opened to the balcony for an hour or so. I guess she enjoyed it; it seems Mom's becoming less and less aware of her surroundings, or maybe it's that she's less demonstrative. That sparkling enthusiasm is harder to see, I suppose, although she did rally a big "hurrah" gesture when Lynn appeared (Lynn got this reaction twice, in fact, in the span of a few minutes). Mostly, Mom would begin a thought, only to drift off before she could conclude it.

Lance and I sang "Keep your Sunny Side Up" to her and Lance even drew illustrations on the white board, but Mom was underwhelmed, in a word. She's still in there, I am sure; it's just harder for her to muster the strength to verbalize her thoughts.

Despite it all, Mom did manage to smile for this photo Lance took of us, during one of her brief moments of lucidity. I'm pleased to report that she slept well. We will see what today brings.

Keep your sunny sides up,

xxoo Mom and Cindy

ANYTHING IS POSSIBLE— NOVEMBER 17, 2014

Happy Monday from the Mouse House,

It was a pretty quiet day here yesterday. Mom had very little to eat, and, unfortunately, had more pain than she's had in awhile. Through it all, she is Mom. She gave me a big smile the first time she saw me and, when I said

"Good morning, how are you?" she said,

"Fine thanks, how are you?"

Actually, come to think of it, that exchange is probably the longest coherent conversation that we have had in days.

Otherwise, Mom was sleepy but restless. She wanted to know if we were upstairs or downstairs, because she needed to go upstairs to put on her dress. It occurs to me that it's been decades since Mom lived in a house with more than one floor and it's been many weeks since she wore anything other than her nightie. When she pleaded the umpteenth time ("pretty, pretty, PRETTY PLEASE") to get up, Tracey and I sat with Mom on the side of the bed. It takes two of us, one on each side, to hold her so that Mom can sit upright. Her feet didn't touch the floor (which she's never liked) and she was squirming and wriggling around, trying to inch her way to the floor—to make a dash for it, I am sure.

"Excuse me please, excuse me," she said to us many times, hoping we'd get out of her way so that she could skedaddle.

"Let's just sit here for a while," I said.

I grabbed some photo albums from her voluminous collection, and we sat on the edge of the bed and looked at those for a time. I wasn't sure if she knew what we were looking at, although at one point she said "Moonglow" while looking at photos of the boat she and Jack once called home. Apparently that activity tired Mom out enough that she abandoned her thoughts of escape and went back to sleep for a bit.

Mom did ask once yesterday, "Where's Dada?"

I told her I didn't know and she seemed to accept that.

Mom frequently looks around with great intent; I know that something's on her mind, but she can't quite verbalize it, which seems to frustrate her. That's frequently when Mom wants to get up and DO something. She had one of those looks last evening, after eating only a very few bites of dinner.

"Uh oh," I thought, "she's getting ideas about bolting just as Tracey is getting ready to leave."

Instead, after looking intently at something I couldn't see, she said,

"I think I will take care of that next year; now I am going to take a little nap."

Phew. But imagine: "next year"? Mom, who always took the bull by the horns and did what needed to be done, is putting something off until *next year*? Wow!

Mom's files are filled with inspirational quotes, stories, columns, etc. A major theme of course is *carpe diem*—going for it, now, while you can. She certainly lived that way and did her best to pass it along to the four of us.

Over the years, Mom has sent countless articles to me—and the boys, too, I'm quite sure. One that I love and have saved in my own special files is entitled "Anything is Possible." I found her copy in the files marked "Copies sent to the kids, 10/92." It's Mom in a nutshell, as she might say—about going for it, now; pursuing your passion, following your heart, dreaming big. It begins:

> IF THERE WAS EVER A TIME TO DARE, TO MAKE A DIFFERENCE, TO EMBARK ON SOMETHING WORTH DOING, IT IS NOW....YOU OWE IT TO YOURSELF TO MAKE YOUR DAYS HERE COUNT.

So that's it for now from the Mouse House. Mom sure did make her days here count.

xxoo C

So Far Life has Been Happy Indeed—November 18, 2014

Good Morning One and All,

It was another quiet day at the Mouse House.

In speaking with Kirk yesterday morning, he was surprised when I told him that there was no way I could explain to Mom why I was going to be out for a couple of hours. (Kirk and Sharon generously let me drive their car while I have been here. Sharon flew in yesterday. So I drove to Ft. Myers, met Sharon and turned over the car—oh, no, poor choice of words—and picked up a rental car). I didn't even attempt to tell Mom where I was going; those conversations just don't work anymore.

It's been days, if not weeks since Mom and I have had any kind of coherent conversation. As mentioned the other day, one exchange like, "Fine thank you, how are you" is about it. Mom spoke very little yesterday, though she was awake most of the day, her eyes darting around the room for a while, and then closing again. That noggin' was clearly churning away. When Lance and Lynn arrived for a visit, she offered a sleepy smile but not much else, although she did ask Lance what he was drinking and mentioned that she thought Lynn looked cold.

Earlier, out of the blue, she'd said to me,

"Is there something I could do to make you feel better?"

So sweet, so heartbreaking... once a mom, always a mom.

Despite being mostly non-responsive, Mom is clearly still in there somewhere, as exhibited by her disappointment when Lance and Lynn left the room when a nurse arrived to examine Mom. Lynn assured her that they'd be back, and that seemed to please her. These few exchanges were Mom's only words all day. I don't even recall that there was much of the disjointed talk or questions about time and where we were, which have been so frequent recently. She ate next to nothing, but still drinks several sips of water over the course of the day.

Sadly, although the nurses turn her frequently, Mom's bed sores are getting worse. The nurse recommended we reconsider using the "moving mattress" gizmo that Mom disliked so much the first time she tried it. We will see; she's in quite different shape both physically and mentally than she was the last time. Wish us luck! I will not go into the somewhat gory details about the bedsores, but they can become open wounds and, given Mom's MDS and lack of red blood cells, there's a concern that if she begins to bleed, her blood will not clot.

Mom must've been awake when I crawled into my bed next to hers last evening. She waved at me, and I waved back. Just two girls having a sleepover. Despite the situation, I feel so lucky to be able to be here with her now. She groaned some during the night, but a small dose of the morphine seemed to ease whatever discomfort she was having and, after that, she slept comfortably. Yay!

We now turn to October 14, 1963. Mom is 39—only a year or so older than Jessica is today. Kirk recently turned 5, and Scott is 11. The family has apparently just moved to Palm Beach, Australia (the place on the beach outside Sydney where we lived before moving to Turramurra). The glimpse we get into the life and times of AKS today comes from a daily diary-type letter that Mom wrote to Dad about those early Australia days, when he was away on business. Reading this, it's hard to imagine how Mom found the time and energy to write at the end of her busy, crazy days. We were new to Australia, didn't know a soul and Dad was off in the Far East somewhere, I assume.

So here's Mom, chauffeuring us around, trying to get us into various schools, shopping for uniforms, and making a picnic to take to the beach. In one day's entry she reported that she bought new beach toys, opened a new bank account, washed the clothes and hung them up, played Scrabble, supervised the boys burning the trash (!) and shined shoes. Later, the boys made a cake and Mom fed us a dinner that

> "the kiddies liked... lamb chops, new potatoes, lettuce and great chocolate cake."

Later entries include things like,

> "Oven conked out yesterday," "I think Cindy has the chicken pox," "Cold all day despite three piece wool suit and now sore throat," and "So far life has been happy indeed."

And my favorite line—only a few lines below: "Children excellent," reported matter-of-factly at the end of the October 14, 1963, entry: "Lance's tooth socked out by Kirk."

Note the use of passive voice... Wonder what it was like when the children *weren't* excellent?

So far, life has been happy indeed.

Love to all, C

With Dad in Turramurra, outside Sydney, Australia circa 1964

Good Morning from the Mouse House and Manila— November 19, 2014

Greetings All,

Another quiet day yesterday at the Mouse House. After many unsuccessful attempts to rouse Mom for breakfast, Brenia and I finally got a few bites into her around mid-day. Mom was very sleepy, nodding off between bites. She did rally a bit when Lance and Lynn came to visit, including asking Lance if he was going to Mt. Kisco (the town next to Bedford Village, New York, where Kirk was born, for you G3'ers). She was a bit more awake when Sharon visited a little later, though it's hard to know how much she understood.

Later, I made the mistake of writing "Are you ready for dinner?" on the whiteboard. Mom got a panicked look on her face and, from her comments, I realized that the answer was "NO!"—she hadn't even made dinner yet and she wasn't dressed.

I convinced Mom that was okay, we had it covered. Next, she wanted to know why she was eating now.

"It's dinnertime."

"Have you eaten?" she challenged me.

"Yes," I lied.

Boy, you should have seen the look I got. She knew that was a whopper.

Next, I thought she asked me what we were eating and I told her it was turkey (tiny bites, almost pulverized). "No, *where* are we eating?" she wanted to know. "In the Mouse House," I answered, knowing that "in bed" would not be well received.

This was much more animated than she'd been all day. In fact, when I walked into her room a bit later and said "Hi!" she asked what I'd said.

"I said 'hi'," I answered at the top of my voice.

"And I said 'hi' back," was her reply.

As Mom was finally going to sleep last night, she called me in a frightened voice to tell me that there was smoke coming in the door from the balcony. (There wasn't, nor was there anything I could see that looked like smoke). It took some convincing, but I calmed her down and she slept pretty well all night.

No sign of the moving mattress yesterday; I will have to follow up with hospice this a.m.

The picture below comes from the June 5, 1965, *Manila Times*[6], taken at a party where Mom and Dad were the honorees at a "Welcome to the Philippines Bario Fiesta." I can't be certain, but I believe that was the party where Mom, as the guest of honor, was given the best seat in the house: front and center at a cock fight. You can imagine Mrs. Shearer's dilemma: she had to feign delight at having this great privilege bestowed upon her, while two nasty roosters fought to the death at her feet.

---

6 Reprinted with the permission of the *Manila Times* where the photograph appeared originally.

FIESTA HONOREES

D. K. Shearer, newly appointed general manager of Colgate-Palmolive Philippines Inc., and Mrs. Shearer were honored at a "Welcome to the Philippines barrio fiesta" given by F. J. Zeitvogel, assistant general manager of Colgate-Palmolive Philippines Inc. and Mrs. Zeitvogel at their home.

I know from Mom's early childhood stories of having to fetch the eggs from the chicken coop that she's not a big fan of fowl. Describing this chore, she'd scrunch up her face and say,

"They sat there with their beady little eyes and I had to reach under them and take their eggs while they squawked and pecked at me."

This clipping is taken from a "Manila" folder that is overflowing with guest lists from the many parties hosted by Mom and Dad while in the Philippines; it was part of Dad's job description—how fitting is that? I can see the parties in my mind's eye, complete with tiki torches in the backyard and the bonka (?) boat floating in the pool. Mom was responsible for coordinating and orchestrating these snazzy affairs—a tall order for a little gal from Hunters Run.

Once again, thanks to all for your feedback. Mom's 'journal' from Australia made a big hit (or should I say a big sock?). Uncle Charley suggested that after "children excellent," an editorial comment of "Mom frazzled" might have been inserted. Indeed.

That's it from chilly Naples—though I guess I'm not going to get much sympathy from the northern contingent.

Love to all, C

NIGHT OFF FOR THE NIGHT SHIFT—NOVEMBER 20, 2014

Okay, well not the *whole* night. But Lance and Lynn kindly stayed with Mom last evening while I went out on the town. Fay had an extra ticket for the Naples Players and invited me to join her group for dinner on Fifth Avenue and the play, "Spitfire Grill." It was a wonderful respite, but that late night (relatively speaking) caused me to sleep in, so you are in luck—today's update will be brief.

Mom was much the same yesterday as she's been; mostly sleepy, interspersed with moments of lucidity and humor. And those amazing sleepy smiles. She's still Mom, through and through—when I asked her,

"Can I borrow your shoes tonight," the answer was,

"Yes, you *MAY!*"

A quickie from the archives, taken from a letter Mom wrote in 1961 to Frances Scott (our *au pair* in Bedford Village, New York, where we lived before moving overseas). It seems like Mom is writing to Frances before she'd accepted the position. Mom describes Bedford Village and our home on Bayberry Lane, emphasizing that there is an automatic washer and dryer and dishwasher. As to the family, she writes:

... My husband and I have college degrees and are outgoing by nature. Our family life is simple and informal with very little pomp and circumstance. We share your interests in swimming and reading and have recently become boating enthusiasts.... The two older children are boys: Scott, 9, and Lance, 7. They also love swimming and reading and are great sports enthusiasts as well as excellent school students. *[wishful thinking?]* The younger children are Cindy, 4½, and Kirk, almost 3. Cindy is sweet and feminine *[definitely wishful thinking]* and Kirk is a lively rascal whom we all thoroughly enjoy.

[Well, she got that part right, though doesn't that make him sound a bit like the family pet?]

Mom and the not quite so Fearsome Foursome in Bedford Village NY circa 1961

Okay, so I think it's time for audience participation. Seems like these morning musings have turned into a tribute to the amazing adventures of AKS, so if anyone would like to share a favorite AKS remembrance, please pipe up.

Signing off from the Mouse House with love to all, C.

LIFE IS BUT A DREAM—
NOVEMBER 21, 2014

Happy Friday from the Mouse House. Once again, Mom slept most of the day. She seemed to be comfortable for the most part. She called Tiva's name a couple of times, so we put a few of his treats into Mom's upturned palm on the bed to lure him to her. Lance tried his best to engage Mom (and we all know how tough he can be to resist) but I think the only thing she said to him was, "Where *is* everybody?"

Despite Mom's sleepiness and lack of verbal communication, she's still trying to engage. She'd point a finger toward the closet and start asking something—and then her eyes would close and she'd drift off. "I'm going to fix that when I get up," she told me a bit later; whatever "that" was...

"Are you hungry?" I often ask, only to get a question in return:

"Are you?"

Mom still wants to take care of me...

A word about Mom's files: You may remember how busy Mom always said she was over the past several months—or even years—staying up till all hours "working on my files," a seemingly endless task. Mom's project was the daunting task of organizing a lifetime's worth of photos, clippings, cards and other memorabilia, which she had lovingly kept and moved countless times. Most of these treasures went around the world. Mom often remarked that "no one is going to care about this stuff once I am gone." I think she would get a large charge out of how much we are enjoying the various glimpses of her life offered up in these files.

Today's glimpse comes from one of the last additions to the AKS files, in the form of a letter that Dana wrote to Mom last month. In her letter, Dana highlights certain recollections of special times with "Grandma and Jack", and describes some of the things she learned from Mom:

> You taught me strength of character, snappy dressing, the art of hostessing, grace, the importance of an adventurous spirit, storytelling, how to eat with chopsticks, bravery, (these two were sometimes combined depending on the international nature of the cuisine), the importance of family, compassion, attention to detail....

Dana goes on to cite several specific recollections:

> Whether you were hosting 2 or 22 at your house, you always looked like you were having **fun** and had it all together...

> I will *never* forget the one-of-a-kind way you tell stories. From the smile you get, to the way your hands gesture and float across the air, jingling your charm bracelet, with a few "you see's" sprinkled about, your matter-of-factness, the way you crack yourself up, the way your perfectly polished nails wipe the lipstick from the corners of your mouth...

Handing out Christmas gifts to "Super Baby" and "Mr. Wonderful" was a treat. What a life together. What love.

There's lots more great reminiscing—the letter is here for perusal when we are all together at Christmastime.

Thanks, Dana for letting me share these great remembrances.

That's it from the Mouse House. A new day has begun. Embrace it. I wish Mom could do so… Though being Mom, I know that she will do her best despite her circumstances.

Love to all, C

JUST LET A SMILE BE YOUR UMBRELLA—NOVEMBER 22, 2014

Happy Saturday from the Mouse House. The pattern continues; Mom sleeps more and more, and when she begins to speak, she just can't muster the energy to complete her thought. She still comments on visitor's outfits, and tells everyone how pretty they look. When Sharon stopped by yesterday wearing a black and white striped top, Mom said, "Everywhere I've been in the last week, people are wearing black and white."

What I wouldn't give to be able to see inside her mind and know where she's "been." Wherever it is, I hope she's happy there... Although, sadly, I think she's still busy. I hear lots of snippets of thought revolving around "fixing that later" and "taking care of it tomorrow." She told us yesterday that she was *SO* sleepy, hadn't slept for weeks and wanted to get home so that she could get some good sleep. Metaphors abound.

When she's more alert, she's still herself, wanting to get up, wanting to know what's around every corner.

"What's in there?" she asks again, pointing into the closet.

"What's out there?" pointing to the living room.

Next, those legs start scooting across the bed, and I know what's coming. She's forgotten that she can't walk and is ready to make her escape. It seems cruel to try to remind her that she can't walk and I doubt that she'd understand, so instead I tell her it's time to sleep. Other times, we get her up to sit in the wheelchair for a bit.

When I got back from a visit with Lance and Lynn last evening, Brenia had Mom up in the wheelchair, and she sat at the kitchen counter for a while and ate a few bites of dinner (mostly creamy pie filing). The nice picture below captures her big outing. At one point—I can't recall why—Mom told Brenia that she was going to pour her water over Brenia's head. We laughed and you should have seen the grin on Mom's face.

Later, from bed, Mom called me frantically and said,

"That is going to boil over," pointing at the balcony door.

"I will take care of it," I told her, and I did so.... Nothing boiled over. Phew!

Another interesting, random comment came earlier in the day when Mom woke up and said quite clearly,

"The opera house is too big."

Boy that mind covers a lot of ground!

From the Life and Times of AKS, here's a glimpse of her early days in her own words, penned for that course she loved about autobiography writing:

> The word that must be used to describe that heterogeneous family that I grew up in is "supportive." Little Adele sang a solo in church while standing on a chair at age 3. Not-much-bigger-Adele did the Gettysburg Address (and all those) at special programs. Also sang "Let a Smile be Your Umbrella" at showers, etc.
>
> But most of all, school came first. My father and mother were keenly interested in my studies and every night after supper was homework time. I *HAD* to be the best in my class. In those days students were ranked scholastically and each month you can imagine who had to be number one. One month Richard Fahnestock tied me at number one and I immediately proceeded to work harder. Never did that happen again.
>
> Even the extracurricular activities were must do's. There was a competition one year – the best picture of Mount Holly

Springs School. "But Monnie," I pleaded, *[using the name she and Aunt Jo called Grandma]* "I can't draw." That's what I thought. I drew and I drew and guess who got the prize. Second best was not acceptable in our world.

[I recall from an earlier update that Mom was 11 at the time; she has the pencil drawing of the school in her amazing files!]

My wonderful Pampaw *[her grandfather]* could hardly wait to see if my Carlisle High School debate team won the state championship in Reading, Pennsylvania that night. We did and he stayed awake to hear the good news. And that night he died. By my senior year I was going to be swamped with the after- school curricular activities, debate team, editor of the weekly newspaper, etc. We lived 10 miles from Carlisle and Hunters Run had no bus service. No problem. We'll just close up the big Hunters Run house for Adele's senior year and move to the little house across the street from the high school. Adele's dates were not too happy with the scratchy horsehair furniture, but "c'est la vie."

Supportive!

My guess is that, though those beaus may not have liked the furniture, they were probably thrilled not to be hitchhiking back and forth to Hunters Run. So that's this morning's Mouse House missive. Enjoy your day, think of Mom, and smile.

xxoo C

ALL ABOARD!—NOVEMBER 23, 2014

Good Morning from the Mouse House,

Another mostly quiet day yesterday. We had a surprise visit from Kirk, who flew in unexpectedly for Thanksgiving.

Sadly, Mom was very groggy while Kirk and Sharon were here. Kirk did get a bit of a smile out of her but, frankly, I'm not sure it registered that it was Kirk and/or that he had just arrived in town. Mom did ask him, "Where is everybody?" (A question that's been asked a lot recently.)

I can't be sure, but I think that she's still looking for the party-goers.

Mom's most animated moment with Kirk was when she opened her eyes and caught him with a toothpick in his mouth—she didn't say anything, but you can imagine the look: her facial expression clearly indicated her disdain… Yes, she's still in there.

Mom ate and drank a bit yesterday, although we didn't get any food into her until almost noon, when we had to rouse her to feed her at least enough that she could tolerate her medicine. Mom spent an hour or so out of bed in conjunction with the sheets being changed. It offered a little variation for her and is preferable to rolling Mom from side to side (to side to side) to accomplish this task while she's in the bed.

The highlight of the day was the arrival of Lance and Lynn with the fiber optic Christmas tree. I must confess I had told Lance that it probably wasn't worth the effort to bring it over, since Mom has become increasingly less aware of her surroundings (with the exception of visitors' clothing and toothpicks...). Boy was I wrong! When Lance plugged the tree in, Mom lit up like... well, you know. What a smile!

"For *me*? From *you*?" she asked Lance incredulously.

I don't know who beamed more, Mom or Lance. It was an extraordinary moment.

"Is it a present for the party?" she asked at one point. She could hardly believe her good fortune.

"It's for *me*," she told me.

I must admit that I've been chagrinned at how early the Christmas season seems to have begun this year; or maybe it's that the thought of Christmas without Mom is unfathomable.

Anyway, the tree was a grand slam, out of the park, walk-off home run. High fives, Lancer.

And now, more autobiographical material. Here's Mom writing about her decision to move the family to Australia in 1963:

> What had I done? I had opened our old Encyclopedia Britannica to the listing "Australia." Two skinny, scary, aborigines were staring up at me.
>
> It was too late to change my mind. I had persuaded my husband that moving our young family overseas was a brilliant way to expand their horizons. His great new job would cover the whole Far East

but home would be in Sydney. Sydney, Australia.

In just a few weeks we'd be sailing off on a ship bigger than we'd ever seen across the blue Pacific on the cruise of our lifetimes. Dad's company had supplied us with reams of information concerning what we would need to pack for "Down Under."

I found a battered old steam trunk with drawers–lost for many years in Stone Lodge's gigantic attic–and packed away: stacks of underwear for my four kiddos aged 5, 7, 9 and 11; 18 pairs of shoes for me (I like shoes), and on and on. We'd be well equipped.

But *aborigines*? What had I **done?**

I can't imagine taking the four of us around the block at ages 5,7, 9 and 11, and here's Mom, persuading Dad to move us half way around the world. And who but AKS could finagle the trip so that we'd travel by train from NY to LA and then via ocean liner (as they were called then) to Australia by way of Tahiti, Bora Bora, etc. (Mom always said the boys—which in those days meant Scott and Lance—requested the train trip, but I'm sure she was tickled pink, too, to borrow her phrase.)

From Mom's notes, I know that the train stopped in Harrisburg and the whole Carlisle contingent showed up on the platform for quick goodbyes. We also stopped for a longer time in Chicago (perhaps to change trains? Boys, help me out here) and visited with family friends who lived there. Next stop was LA and Disney Land, before boarding the SS *Monterey* for the cruise of our lifetimes.

No wonder Mom's tired! Enjoy your day and don't take no for an answer!

CINDY SHEARER, who arrived with her parents, Mr and Mrs D. K. Shearer, formerly of Bedford Village, New York, and her three brothers, in the Monterey yesterday. The family intends to settle in Sydney.

xxoo

"WE HAD ALWAYS WANTED TO GO THERE, SO NOTHING WAS GOING TO STOP US"—NOVEMBER 24, 2014

Good Morning.

That quintessential AKS line comes from another of Mom's autobiography class assignments, describing Mom and Dad's honeymoon destination, Bermuda. It captures her sense of adventure and travel, combined with her trademark tenacity. But before we get to the honeymoon stage, check out some of her recollections about earlier interests...

Boys? Yea. I started looking them over in third grade. David Wilcox, with freckles, in Clearwater Florida. He was adorable. Next big memory: Buddy Snead, also in Clearwater. He had a red convertible. But that's when our family returned north on a full-time basis. And I became forever mad for convertibles.

Now I was at Carlisle High and began my first job for the *Carlisle Evening Sentinel*. The pay was paltry (five cents a column inch) but the staff there was great fun and all male.

Don Englander invited me to the junior prom but I hadn't learned to dance. "No problem," he said, "I'll teach you." So I learned. My Mother made my first formal; fuchsia taffeta, long with black velvet straps and a short matching jacket with black velvet buttons. I can see it now.

But would you believe the most memorable moment of my teenage years was choosing my husband? It's true. When I spotted this great looking guy who knew all the answers in 11th grade journalism class I knew immediately. The year was 1939. We never dated in high school.

The next male in my life was Paul Boyle, a handsome, blonde Irishman. We dated pretty steadily through our senior year. He survived the black, scratchy horsehair while waiting for me in the living room chairs or sofa that came with the rental house my family moved into across the street from the high school to manage my extracurricular extravaganzas during that senior year... But this relationship ended when my time in high school ended.

[So she says... though I recall stories about a handsome beau who travelled to visit her at Ursinus College with an engagement ring in his pocket, and all the girls thought she was mad not to go for him. If this wasn't Paul, who was it??]

Also ending was my editorship of the school newspaper. Don Shearer had been chosen to take over from me.

That summer my guy hitchhiked 10 miles out of Carlisle to my house in Hunters Run. No movies, no out-to-dinners. We hiked on the Appalachian Trail, played croquet, walked on stilts and all those good things, and we could cuddle in front of the fireplace. My family liked him too and often invited him to stay for dinner. Sometimes he would stay overnight. Later that summer my family invited him to accompany me, my sister and my parents on a two-week automobile tour through New England. Who could ask for anything more?

Don was a year younger. That meant he was staying behind for his senior year at Carlisle High while I was off to spend my freshman year at Ursinus College. I was far too involved with my extracurriculars to pay much attention to the V-12'ers who were assigned to Ursinus after the original male freshmen were sent off to war, following Pearl Harbor. Don enlisted immediately in the Army Air Corps and stood by to be assigned. (*If I recall correctly, Dad lied about his age in order to enlist, and ended up as the youngest member of a B-17 crew that flew bombing missions over Germany*).

My guy did safely come home from the war and in the fall of the following year, after my graduation, my chosen one and

I said our vows amidst hundreds of red
poinsettias covering the First Lutheran
Church in Carlisle, Pennsylvania, on
December 21, 1946. It was the longest
night of the year.…

Our wedding trip was to Bermuda. We had
always wanted to go there, so nothing
was going to stop us. We pooled our
paltry resources and off we went. We
even lucked into an extra day. We were
flying by seaplane and the Baltimore
Harbor was frozen over on our scheduled
day to return to the United States. The
bridegroom returned to college and I got
back to my editor's job editing the Army
Information School Cavalcade.

Below is a photograph from Mom and Dad's wedding album.[7] Mom
hated the photos in the album and really took me to task for showing
the album to the assembled gang a couple of Christmases ago.

---

7   In deference to Mom, that photo is not reprinted here; instead I've
included one of Mom and Dad from the late 1960's.

If I remember correctly, Mom said that she and Dad had worked very hard and slept very little in the days leading up to the wedding and she thought they both looked awful in their wedding photos. Among other things, they had pulled all-nighters (did they call them that then?) to prepare their "Town Talk" newspaper columns in advance, given the upcoming honeymoon.

Fast forward 68 years... Mom is much the same as reported in recent days; resting, if not sleeping, pretty much all day. Her pain is thankfully infrequent and seems to respond well to the morphine.

As if to confirm my suspicion that her mind is all over the map, so to speak, she said to me from bed yesterday,

"I just want to go to bed."

Poor thing—whatever she's up to, it's exhausting.

Several times as I sat next to her yesterday, she'd open her eyes for a moment, see me and talk to me from the middle of her dream-like state. These comments included,

"Do they cook those in a pan?"…

"Don't let those things get beaten up."…

"Is she selling them?"…

"*You're* baking?" (pointing at me).

"*I'm* baking."…

"Is the staff eating now?"…

And my favorite:

"I just told you that."

Mom continues commenting on outfits (she asked how many buttons were on my shirt and admired my color combination).

This morning has been a bit dicey. Seems like the catheter is leaking— again. Wish us luck.

Love to all, xxoo C

THE FIVE MINUTE LOUVRE
LADY—NOVEMBER 25, 2014

Good Morning All,

Yesterday was tough and, if I truly want to portray what's going on here—which was my initial reason for writing these updates—I must share with you the tough times as well as the laughs and memories.

Poor Mom. Her mind is going a million places at the same time, which exhausts her. She asked me for a paper and pencil yesterday, to write me a note. I reminded her that she doesn't need to write to me—I can hear her.

Mom gets confused about this at times, since I write notes to her. She insisted on writing to me; it seemed that she had something very important to tell me, and she wanted to memorialize it in writing. I brought her a pencil and paper and she wrote, slowly and deliberately, in very shaky but decipherable capital letters:

"I MUST REST."

Amazing. This from someone who hasn't been out of bed for more than a few hours in the last several weeks. You'd think we'd been asking her to run marathons. The hospice folks and literature describe this restless state. Jennifer, the hospice nurse, says that Mom is probably busy tying up loose ends. Mom's head was certainly busy again yesterday and, unlike previous days, she spoke frequently, but still in the disjointed manner I've tried to describe:

"I need to get up and make some phone calls."…

"I need to go buy something for dinner."…

"I am nowhere else other than here, am I?"…

"We are here now and tomorrow we go to school?"

These random remarks were spoken at intervals, with lots of what appeared to be dozing in between them. As the day progressed, Mom became more and more anxious, thrashing around, trying to pull out her catheter, calling for Jack, and asking who the man was standing by her bed.

"Cindy I don't know what I am doing," she remarked at one point.

After a particularly tough period of groaning and thrashing around, she quieted down and said,

"I love you darling," to me (or perhaps to someone else who I couldn't see).

Mom didn't want any dinner and, just as I thought she was finally drifting off to sleep, Mom asked,

"Is this the Thames? Is this the Thames River?"

I said, "Yes, it is," which was apparently the wrong answer, as it set off a panicky, frantic request for me to call 9-1-1.

This went on for some time. I would tell Mom that there was no emergency, everything was fine and she'd challenge me:

"How do you know? What makes you so sure?"

Try explaining how you know there's no emergency to someone who's unable to reason.

When she gave up on me, she started in on Brenia:

"Bring me the phone. How do you call 9-1-1 from overseas?" (Are we in London?)

And so on. Poor Mom. Did I mention she isn't known for taking "no" for an answer?

Mom finally settled down, with the help of some morphine, but was wide awake again at midnight, wanting to get up. Would I please, please, *please* take her to school? I tried to find out what school, with no luck. Then Mom wanted me to find a janitor to get something down from somewhere. I told her it was the middle of the night; there wasn't a janitor to be found. Ever skeptical, Mom persisted.

"Just waltz out there and see if you can't find one," she begged.

Next she wanted to know where the police station was and asked if I could take her to the train station.

Having gotten nowhere trying to persuade Mom that she needed to sleep, I tried another angle, and appealed to her maternal instincts.

"I need to sleep," I told her.

That didn't seem to sink in, but with the help of another dose of morphine, she thankfully fell back to sleep, although she talked sporadically in her sleep most of the night. Still busy.

How exhausting it all must be. How I wish she could rest peacefully. How odd to want her suffering to be over, despite what I know that will mean.

On a happier note, here's a glimpse into Mom's busy life. It's an itinerary for Mrs. Adele Shearer, typed on a 5 x 7 card, for the period 7/27 - 8/22. Sadly, no year. But fasten your seat belts, because this is where Mom went during that approximately three week time period:

```
JFK- HONOLULU
HONOLULU-TOKYO
TOKYO-HONG KONG
HONG KONG-MANILA
MANILA-BANGKOK
BANGKOK-KUALA LUMPUR
KUALA LUMPUR-SINGAPORE
SINGAPORE-SYDNEY
SYDNEY-HONOLULU
HONOLULU-LOS ANGELES
LOS ANGELES-NEW YORK JFK
```

Phew. No grass under her feet.

It reminds me of the shakedown cruise on *Moonglow* that Kevin and I did with Mom and Jack in Desolation Sound, British Colombia, in 1992. Jack and Kevin would look at the chart and say,

"We can go here today, or we can go there."

Mom would study the chart, ask what time sunset was, what our maximum speed was, and how far we could travel before needing to refuel, and then she'd somehow finagle it so that we could go both here *and* there that day. Mom comes by the moniker "The Five Minute Louvre Lady" honestly.

At the same time, as that well-known poet Kirk Shearer noted recently, she also tried to instill in us the importance of not letting life pass us by. Kirk wrote to Mom:

```
Roses are red,
Violets are blue,
I love to smell the flowers
And it's all because of you.
```

Signing off from the Mouse House. Love to you all.

xxoo

Thanksgiving Eve Morning at the Mouse House—November 26, 2014

Hi Everybody,

Last night was awful. Mom had what I can only think to describe as a psychotic incident. She wasn't on any meds at the time and I have no idea what triggered it. I was very shaken and scared and am not able to write about it, at least not now. Frankly I wish I could forget it and see little point in burdening all of you with the memory, too.

Fortunately, with the help of 2 TCG gals, we got Mom calmed down and she had her first dose of her new anti-anxiety medicine. Thankfully, she slept soundly after that. I am sure she was exhausted; I was.

The day began routinely. Mom rested most of the day and was uncharacteristically chatty when Lance, Lynn and Carly arrived around 4:30. It was great to have them here and we ended up ordering pizza and eating it in the Mouse House. Finally, someone's shown up for the party! Mom was lucid, at one point asking me if I'd served everyone their pizza. Later, she pointed outside at something that caught her eye.

"Look!" she said, excitedly, glimpsing out her balcony door in the same direction where she frequently "sees things."

"A Christmas tree," I ventured, because we could see one in the window on the other side of the courtyard.

"No," she said, pointing emphatically. (She didn't add "you fool," although her tone made it clear that's what she was thinking).

And sure enough, there it was, a crescent moon hanging in the little piece of sky that Mom can see from her bed.

Carly, who like her grandmother never misses a beat, said immediately,

"The moon was at the top of her list of favorite things!"

Despite these glimpses of clarity, Mom was also a little loopy. I placed some treats for Tiva in her hand, to lure him to her. Bad move; Mom tried to put them in her mouth. I took the treats from her, but she continued to mime the action of eating things out of her hand. Speaking of hands, Mom's hands and arms flutter all over the place, whether she's sleeping or awake. Sometimes, it's as if she's reaching for something, and sometimes it's as if she's conducting an orchestra or playing cat's cradle with an invisible playmate. Maybe she figures if she can't get anywhere with her legs, she will use her arms instead.

Today's offering from the Life and Times of AKS is a painting that she made while taking an art class in Australia. That she had time to do so is remarkable in itself, given the laundry list (pun intended) of tasks she faced, caring for her four "excellent kiddies."

The painting, she thinks, is of a scene from Nova Scotia. It is on loan to the Mouse House from the AKS Gallery located in Kirk and Sharon's master bath. She told Kirk recently that she was unhappy with two things about her painting—the size of the boatman's head, and the unfinished piece next to the tree. As a benchmark of sorts, I recall talking to Mom about this painting when I arrived here less than a month ago. The conversation we had then is one that we could never have today. Another AKS *carpe diem* lesson.

Love to all. Happy Thanksgiving Eve.

xxoo C

HAPPY THANKSGIVING FROM THE
MOUSE HOUSE—NOVEMBER 27, 2014

Good Morning and Happy Thanksgiving to all,

The first thing on my list of things that I am thankful for on this Thanksgiving morning is the fact that Mom slept quietly and calmly all night, appearing to be getting some good, deep sleep. When I spoke to the hospice nurse about Mom's episode the night before, she assured me that it was not unusual at this stage. (Oh great, how reassuring!) The nurse mentioned something called "sleep psychosis," which I Googled and learned that it is a condition where lack of sleep can cause delusional behavior.

It's been clear for some time that, while she's in bed pretty much around the clock, Mom is not really resting—at least her mind is not. "Going a mile a minute," I can hear her say, although my money's on several miles a minute. She's even realized it and committed it to writing the other morning in her "I MUST REST" note; most likely her last note to me.

It seems that the new anti-anxiety medicine has calmed Mom's mind as we'd hoped, allowing her to sleep. And, no, to those who've asked teasingly, I haven't tested it myself, at least not yet. ;-). Mom slept virtually all day yesterday; she ate a little bit in the morning and then had a "bed bath"—but she was groggy at best during both events. The only thing I recall her saying to me, late in the afternoon, was,

"Cindy, we can't keep living under these conditions."

How true. "Out of the mouth of babes..." as Mom might say.

I keep forgetting to tell you about a phone call that Mom had with Aunt Jo a few weeks ago. It was the last phone call she could participate in, with me relaying what was said on the other end of the line. (WITH ME RELAYING WHAT WAS SAID ON THE OTHER END OF THE LINE... I SAID, **WITH ME RELAYING WHAT WAS SAID ON THE OTHER END OF THE LINE**). You get the picture. Anyway, even then, it was hard to know how much of the conversation Mom really understood after the "fine thank you, how are you?" part. She was nodding off and her responses were vague, until Aunt Jo explained that Charley wasn't home because he had gone to the shoe repair shop.

"I hope they have enough leather," quipped Mom, without missing a beat.

(For you G3'ers, Uncle Charley has size 13 (?) feet—sorry Charley, if I shouldn't reveal that. Anything for a story).

Aunt Jo and I remarked later how surprised we both were that Mom could seem so out of it and yet come up with such a snappy line on the spot. Looking back, this was the first occasion when Mom seemed to be both present and elsewhere simultaneously.

Maybe that explains Mom's question to me the other day; I don't recall exactly what she said, but it was something like,

"I know we are here, but are we somewhere else, too?"

Apparently, she is.

Remarkable.

Also in this category was an exchange we had a few mornings back, with me writing on the white board:

ME: Are you ready for breakfast?

MOM: Who is breakfast?

ME: (Wow! Okay, let's see…) Are you ready for some eggs?

MOM: Are they soft boiled or poached?

Sophia, one of the many TCG nurses who love Mom, stopped in to see her yesterday. Even though they no longer care for Mom on a regular basis—Brenia and I have taken over those roles for the most part—many of the TCG nurses still come by, wanting to say hello to Mom. It's pretty great. Since Mom was sleeping soundly, Sophia and I chatted for a bit. She told me that TCG has lost four hospice people this week and that Mom was enrolled in hospice before any of them. Oh great, I thought, so now she's going for her final blue ribbon?

Later in the day, the hospice chaplain stopped in. She's the one who a few months ago told Mom that she was there to answer any questions Mom may have, noting that at the end of life people often have questions or concerns they'd like to discuss. Mom "listened" intently (Elaine was using the white board) and when Elaine asked, "Do you have any questions for me?" Mom nodded affirmatively.

I was sure that Mom was going to raise her concern about juggling two husbands in heaven. Instead, Mom said,

"Yes, I do have a question. What is the shade of that lipstick that you are wearing?"

Classic Mom.

Anyhow, when Chaplain Elaine and I were discussing death yesterday, she said something like, "People tend to die like they lived." I buy that in Mom's case. It seems that she's forgotten her strong resolve to die and, instead, her determined "anything-is-possible" personality is kicking in.

As I scour the files for fun tidbits ("Tidbits," by the way, was the name of the newspaper Mom edited in third grade, launching her editorial career), I continue to be struck by the assortment of amazing artifacts that Mom has amassed over the years and how, when viewed as a whole, they capture her essence so well. Today's handful of offerings from the files include a birthday note from her beloved Dada dated April 30, 1945 (her 21st birthday), a long note from Scott apologizing for a fight he and Mom had over use of the car, and another mind-numbing itinerary from April 1974—her wedding trip with Jack. Check this out:

NY-LA-HONOLULU-GUAM-HONG KONG-BANGKOK-
DELHI-KARACHI-TEHRAN-ISFAHAN-SHIRAZ-
KABUL-ISTANBUL-BEIRUT-LONDON-NY.

Also, there is no shortage of notes to and from Jack—beginning in their courting days and continuing through their 30-something anniversary. How smitten they were. A major theme in Jack's notes over the years is how captivated he was by her smile. The same smile that melts me even now, that lights up the room when she opens her eyes and sees me.

Below is a shot taken by Lance that Mom and Jack used as a Christmas card. It's from the late 70's, I'm guessing. They are sitting on the dock with Buff, the golden retriever we got as a puppy in Australia (and who also had a pretty amazing life as a world traveler).

Before signing off—seeing as it's Thanksgiving and all—I want to express my gratitude to everyone who is reading this for your calls, texts, emails, visits, hugs, meals, clothes, chances for a respite from the nightshift—and for all you have done and are doing to allow me to have this precious time with Mom.

Love to all, C

Happy Thanksgiving From The Mouse House—Update November 27, 2014—5:00 P.M.

Greetings.

We are moving Mom to Hospice House today. She is very restless and showing signs of the beginning of the end. I will keep you posted. I love you all.

Good Morning from Hospice House—November 28, 2014

Greetings All,

I am watching the sunrise over the pretty lake outside Mom's window here at Hospice House. A wood stork just soared in and is scrounging for breakfast in the lake. I am more fortunate; last evening, Lance hand-delivered the most amazing Thanksgiving meal with every imaginable trimming, including some of Lance's pumpkin and Carly's pecan pie. So I had pie-times-two for breakfast, accompanied by delicious coffee also provided by Lance.

Yesterday morning started out well at TCG, with Mom wanting to get out of bed. We got her up and gave Mom breakfast at the kitchen counter. She seemed to be fine, although she was not very talkative. In fact, the only clear thing I remember her saying was something like, "I'd like to put my head in that," pointing to her orange juice cup.

Although Brenia and I said and wrote "Happy Thanksgiving" to Mom, it didn't seem to register...but who knows? Anyway, Mom ate a bit of breakfast and, soon after, she began to tremble erratically, as if experiencing an earthquake. Her arms and legs would shake and she would groan, sounding very frightened.

With great difficulty, we got Mom back to bed. At one point, I think she mentioned stairs. Poor Mom, it was as if she thought she was falling—her greatest fear for some time now.

To make a long story not quite so long, after consulting with Nurse Jennifer, who happened to be on duty yesterday (the one holiday of the year that she works—talk about something to give thanks for!), it was decided that Mom's discomfort could no longer be managed at TCG and that she should be moved to Hospice House, where they can evaluate her, increase meds as needed and care for her around the clock.

Jennifer said, "Now you can be the daughter and let others be the nurse." No argument from me!

Mom seemed to sleep soundly last night. (There's a comfy chair here in her room that converts into a bed and I slept soundly, too!) Mom has not been communicating since this episode began yesterday morning, although she did manage a smile for Lance when he came by to say Happy Thanksgiving sometime mid-day. Turns out he got her last smile.

A couple of the TCG nurses stopped by to see Mom when they heard she was being moved. They pointed out changes in her breathing, which indicated to them that Mom's systems were shutting down. When I asked Jennifer if she thought Mom would be returning to the Mouse House, she said she doubted it, estimating that Mom's end would come within a week or so. The TCG nurses seemed to think it may be sooner than that. I have no idea; she's surprised me before, and we all recall how many times Jack bounced back. Anyway, I will be interested to see if she can communicate or eat this morning.

The attached note is one I found not long ago, when looking through Mom's checkbook. She'd clearly stuck it there so that it wouldn't be found until she was gone. Her final treasure hunt treasure... Come to think of it, Mom approached life like a treasure hunt and encouraged us to do the same. Be forewarned, the note is a tear-jerker. Tissues recommended.

> Remember to
> Seize the Day
> I'm seizing this day,
> Sept. 3, 2013, for
> no particular reason
> except that who knows
> how many more days
> I might have.
> I have re-read all
> those decades of
> dear mommy cards &
> letters and realize all
> over again how
> wonderful are my
> fabulous four. You
> made me what I am.
> I love each one of you
> deeply — more than
> I can ever tell you.
> Keep up the good work!

I will try to keep everyone posted going forward, but I think this will be the last of my rambling missives. Or not. If I have learned anything this month, it's the line from the *Pippin* song, "Just No Time at All:"

"If there's one thing to be sure of, mate, there's nothing to be sure of."

(Lance and I sang this number to Mom not too long ago; she was not impressed.) If you don't know it, Google it and take a listen. It captures so much of Mom's life philosophy; the way she lived and the way she encouraged us to live.

Seize the day, smell the roses, and do your best— whatever life poses.

Love to all, C

Epilogue—Mother's Day, 2015

That was my last "official" update. Mom never regained consciousness, as far as I could tell. She died at Hospice House on the Monday after Thanksgiving, at around 3:00 p.m.—in time for us to get to sunset at the beach, one of Mom's favorite activities. It seemed like the perfect way to honor Mom's life and I felt like she was watching it too, from the other side, wherever that may be.

At Christmastime, in accordance with Mom's wishes, we all gathered to celebrate her life and spread her ashes in the Gulf of Mexico, not far from where we'd sprinkled Jack's two years earlier.

After my husband Kevin died, there were so many things that made me think of him. In Mom's case, it's easier to list the things that don't make me think of her.

The sky makes me think of Mom.

"Will you just LOOK at those clouds!" I hear her declare enthusiastically as I gaze upward.

"I defy you to find a funner family," she boasts in my mind's eye during a boisterous Shearer gathering.

Mom often told me that on a clear day, her Mother would wonder "who got up early and shined all the leaves." On a pretty morning, those words play in my head, and I smile at the thought that Mom and Grandma had a hand in polishing the day.

Today is my first Mother's Day without her and, naturally, I miss Mom like crazy. But I am happy that she is no longer suffering and I am determined to seize the day in tribute to her.

I also hope that by sharing this with others, I have honored in a small way Mom's desire that we reconsider how our culture deals with—or fails to deal with—end of life issues.

If she could have done so, I believe that Mom would have taken her own life; she admitted as much. Mom was no quitter; quite the opposite, as I think has been demonstrated in these pages. She had always played by the rules and fully embraced life, and I am sure that it violated every fiber of her being to contemplate such an ending.

However, she was distraught by her inability to participate in life on a meaningful level, and aghast at the thought that she was a burden. Kevin's succinct mantra sums it up pretty well—life is to be enjoyed, not endured.

Thankfully, because of her terminal diagnosis, Mom was able to take some control over her death. Without that, she would have continued to endure an ever-declining quality of life, coupled with an ever-rising cost of supporting that life.

Although I have no answers, I think Mom was absolutely right: there needs to be a better system. As Lance remarked when Jack was dying, we treat our animals better than our people when it comes to the end. As tough as euthanizing our four-legged friends can be, it is so clearly the humane and compassionate thing to do when their quality of life is gone and they are suffering. Surely we can do a better job of ensuring the same dignified ending for our two-legged loved ones.[8]

Fortunately for us, Mom got her wish: to close the last chapter of her extraordinary life on her own terms. Thanks to the magic carpet rides afforded by Mom's fabulous files, we all got to share that chapter with her, in an on-going celebration of her life.

And I got to spend 90 years with Mom in 30 remarkable days. For that, I thank my Mom, my family, and my lucky stars.

---

8   It turns out there are several organizations who are working diligently on a "better system" for end of life care. I found loads of information and helpful forms and checklists online. These groups include: Compassion & Choices (www.compassionandchoices.org); Death with Dignity National Center (deathwithdignity.org);National Hospice and Palliative Care Organization (nhpco.org), Hospice Foundation of America (hospicefoundation.org) and Hospice Action Network (hospiceactionnetwork.org).

Mom and Cindy mid-late 1970's

ACKNOWLEDGEMENTS

I would like to express my gratitude to Brenia, Tracey, Sophia, Barb, Jennifer, Elaine and the rest of the TCG and Avow Hospice crews for your tireless devotion to Mom.

I would like to thank my whole "fam damily" as Mom would say- Joan and Charley, Scott and Alicia, Lance and Lynn, Kirk and Sharon, Jessica and Sean, Jaclynn, Matt and Belle, Becca and Jason, Dana and Ryan, Carly, and honorary family member Fay- for all your love and support.

Thank you Lynn for lovingly assembling and printing my original emails, thereby planting the seed that became this book.

Thank you Carol for encouraging me to spend this last precious time with Mom.

Thank you Sibyl for encouraging me to share my story with others- and for your expert input into design details.

Thanks to the many friends and family members who encouraged me to keep plugging away at this project; to all who read and proofed early drafts, offered comments, nudged me when I needed nudging, and provided invaluable input and insight every step of the way.

Thank you Lucy for your enthusiasm and meticulous copy editing.

Thanks to Gibby, Roxy and Ali for your comic relief.

Last but not least, thanks to my amazing brothers, for your love and support and for sharing the journey every step of the way. I am so glad that we are in this together.

Printed in the United States
By Bookmasters